Every Good Boy Deserves Fruit

Every Good Boy Deserves Fruit

Calvin Corvidian

Gymnopedie

http://www.lulu.com/spotlight/cancorv

Published by Gymnopedie 2013

Copyright © Calvin Corvidian 2013

ISBN 978-1-300-60872-1

Contact

gymnopinfo@gmail.com

Cover design

Marek Procházka

Editor

Anne Johnson

Calvin Corvidian

Having a birthday on February 29th, Calvin is much younger than he looks. He is one of many foreigners living in Brno, the capital of Moravia. His *raison d'être* is writing gay stuff: there is a book of short stories called *Those Czech Boys*, a soon to be completed novel, a drafted novel, and a completed but unpublished first novel from twenty-five years ago, which was probably called *Gymnopedie*. In the virtual world of the 21st century, Calvin has a blog at gymnop.blogspot.com as well as gay e-learning courses in English as a Foreign Language linked on the blog.

Reading this book as a learner of English

The story is set in the Czech Republic around the turn of the century. The main character, Dan, is a Czech university student of German language and literature. But he often has to speak English, which he studied a little at school. In this book, he makes many mistakes speaking English. You can find out about these in the course website. When he is speaking Czech and German, usually expressed in English in this book, he does not make mistakes.

There are many words, phrases, and cultural references that might be new to a learner of English. Each chapter begins with a list of vocabulary. There are also a few notes about cultural references. You can study these and more at the course website.

A learner of English would benefit from reading this book twice. The first time, enjoy the story, the situation and the characters. The second time, study the language that is new and interesting to you: picture the words and phrases in your mind and think about whether they are important or useful for you: make a note of the words you do not know but would like to.

At the website you can study the words and phrases in a number of enjoyable ways. You can talk about the book in general, discuss the characters, and ask about any references which are unclear. You can also answer other readers' questions and discuss their comments.

Buying this book gives you free access to the website. Send an email to gymnopinfo @gmail.com with the User Name you'd like to use, your first and last names, and your email address.

1 Caught in the Act

Vocabulary

balance (vb) **on tiptoes** stand on your toes, heel lifted off the ground, and stay in this position. Try it now!

pubic hair (compound noun) is the hair around the penis (or vagina but not much in this story).

lout (n) a young man who behaves rudely and sometimes violently. Rhymes with *out*.

give someone a **blow job** (vb phrase) suck his penis till he cums.

glare (vb) look at someone in a way that shows you are surprised or angry.

shrink/shrank/shrunk (vb) become smaller like clothes when they are washed for the first time.

sheath (n) a protective covering like a leather knife holder.

flaccid (adj) soft rather than firm /flaksid/ or /flasid/. e.g. muscles, a plant, a penis (a.k.a. dick, cock, member, Johnson, willy, phallus) can be flaccid.

post-coital (adj) after sex, e.g. a post-coital cigarette.

Free Willy a brand of clothing. But "willy" is a slang word for penis, so not wearing underwear (a.k.a. *to go commando*) means that your willy moves freely inside your jeans.

The story begins

Dan chose a CD from the shelves and put it on nice and loud. During the first song, he slowly took all his clothes off and threw them as if in slow motion onto the armchair. When he was naked, he stroked the length of one arm and then the other. His open palms then moved across his chest, down his torso, around his hips, and down his thighs and calves till he was touching his toes. He slowly straightened his whole body as his extended arms drew a wide circle. His fingertips met high above his head and he balanced himself on tiptoes. He remained in this position till the song ended, enjoying his beauty in the long mirror.

While he was dancing with his reflection to the second song, he noticed a magazine on the coffee table. When the song finished, he let himself drop to the floor, then lay on his back with his feet on the seat of the armchair. With one hand he took the magazine, while his other hand played in his thick bush of dark pubic hair. He was still slowly turning the pages when Ivana came out of the bathroom dressed for sex. She took the magazine and tossed it onto the couch.

"Disgusting. Men fucking each other. Horrible."

"No it's not. Have you looked at these photos?"

"No. And don't even ask me to. Phooey."

"Some of them are beautiful. Just art."

She took him by the hand and led him to bed. "Now show me your art."

"God that's good. I love it when you do that." He was teasing her nipples with his tongue. "Don't stop. Please don't stop. Deeper, deeper. Ahhhhhh! You didn't, did you? Oh Dan, that's beautiful. Did you come? Great. You promised you wouldn't. Not inside. Fuck that was good. You promised."

"Sorry. But I just couldn't stop myself. Once I get to that point, something else takes over. Do you still love me?"

A third, much older voice shouted in English. "What the fucking fuck's fuck is going on here? Who the fuck are you? And what the fuck do you think you are doing in my bed, you fucking lout! Get off her." His tone softened as he asked Ivana if she was alright. As they sat up, she held the sheet in front of them and wiped her face with it. She started to apologise, to explain, to say anything. Casey turned to the boy. "And who might you be, young man?"

"Ich zorry," he said, his whole body shaking.

Casey looked back at Ivana and waited for an explanation.

"I'm sorry, Mr. Casey. He's my boyfriend. He's hardly speaking English." Dan thought that was a bit unfair. He'd studied English for four years at school, although his passion had always been for German.

"So you only speak Czech, then?"

"No, he is studying German," Ivana answered for him again.

"You have no right to bring anyone into my flat. I've given you keys for a cleaning job, not a blow job."

Ivana glared at Casey. She rested her hand gently on Dan's shoulder and told him in Czech to get dressed. In shock and embarrassment his cock had shrunk back into its sheath as a tortoise head might under such circumstances. He followed his semi-flaccid post-coital cock across the room. Casey's eyes did likewise. Dan bent over to pick up his clothes from the armchair and flashed them both a good look at his arse. "Bottoms up!" thought Casey.

"Ich gehe," he said, announcing his departure quietly but angrily while slipping on his second-hand pinstripe trousers.

"Free Willy," Casey said to himself.

Dan looked at Ivana as if to say, let's get out of here. She shook her head and said in Czech, "Just go." He buttoned up a loose-fitting 1940s waistcoat, then slipped his trainers on and knelt to tie his shoelaces. He stood up, tousled his hair in the mirror, and through a bitter smile said in Czech, "fucking fag." And left, sadly closing the door behind him.

"I'm sorry, Mr Casey, but there is nowhere else for us to go at the moment. My grandmother moved into our flat recently and she's always in the home."

"She's always *at* home. That is not my problem. You brought a complete stranger into my flat. You were fucking on my bed. You weren't even using condoms, you fucking idiots!"

"We always do it before I wash the sheets."

"So this is not the first time?"

Ivana shook her head slowly and sadly, realising she had said too much. Trying to shift the focus, she said, "You are home very early today."

"Yes, I decided to take the afternoon off and have a game of squash, and then I ... Why am I explaining this to you? You are now finished here. Forever."

Ivana cried, "No! Please Mr Casey, it is not happening again. I promise."

"It will definitely not happen again," he said in a calm but firm voice. "You have betrayed my trust, young lady. More than once. I'd be a fool to trust you again. I'm afraid I have to let you go."

She slowly took hers and Dan's clothes out of the clothes dryer, and folded everything carefully. When she was done, Casey asked for the keys. She pointed to them on the coffee table. She turned and left, sadly closing the door behind her.

2 Dan Returns to the Scene of the Crime

Vocabulary

dressing gown (compound noun) a long loose piece of clothing, like a coat, which you wear informally inside the house, especially at breakfast time.

ponytail (compound noun) when the hair is tied up at the back and hangs down like a horse's tail

knock on the door (fixed phrase) to signal you want to come in.

manual labour (compound noun) work that is physical not mental.

drawer (n) part of a piece of furniture that slides in and out and is used for keeping things in.

crumpled (adj) what happens to clothes which have not been neatly folded.

inhale to breathe in. The opposite is to exhale.

crotch (n) the part of your body where legs meet the torso. May rhyme with either *watch* or *much*.

fault (n) the responsibility for something wrong that has happened. Often: *it is not my fault.*

visible (adj) can be seen.

tight (adj) clothes that are close to your body, sometimes sexy, sometimes uncomfortable.

The doorbell rang. Casey opened the door in his full-length dressing gown and saw Dan with all his thick jet-black hair now tied neatly back in a ponytail.

"I Dan, boyfriend von Ivana." His blue eyes matched the sky perfectly.

"You came here just to remind me of that? Cheers." The coolness in Casey's voice matched that of the early spring morning. Casey closed the door and closed his eyes waiting for the next ring of the doorbell. Dan knocked on the door very loudly. The Englishman opened the door and looked down into those soft blue eyes and waited for him to say something.

Dan took a piece of paper out of his pocket and started to read. "I am very sorry for being in this your nice flat with Ivana. She should be working only there. But I help her one day when she had big test. She show me wall pictures, magazines, and …"

Casey stopped him, stood aside, and showed him in. As Dan bent over to take off his shoes, Casey was reminded of the naked butt that farewelled him three days ago. He pointed to the armchair. Dan sat down and continued. "… and that picture is very liking to me." He pointed to it. "And magazines here is sexy. So I feel sexy. And that is why we sexed here. Ivana said no no no. So I am bad person, not Ivana. Please let her to work here. She work good, no?"

"I don't know," said Casey. "Perhaps you work better."

"Please, she need money. We are students and she has no father. They is very poor. Her grandmother sick too. I make to her problems. Poor Ivana."

"Look, I'm very busy. I'm having visitors tonight. It seems you have time, so why don't you help me clean now? I'll pay you, of course."

"I call Ivana?"

"No. You will work. Let's get started. But first you need to change."

"Change?"

"You can't do manual labour in those clothes." Casey led him into the bedroom, opened a drawer and pulled out a crumpled T-shirt and some jogging shorts. As Casey turned to leave, Dan held the clothes against his face and inhaled deeply. He was surprised to find the smell a bit sexy. Leaving the room, Casey smiled as he caught the boy admiring himself in the mirror.

When Dan joined Casey in the living room, Casey looked him up and down and said, "Yes, you'll do quite nicely, thank you." The words didn't mean anything to Dan, but he understood the way Casey's eyes studied him, and how they returned to his crotch several times. Dan knew that it was his fault for not wearing underwear. He also knew that the shape of his cock was visible through the very tight shorts and he could feel it starting to grow.

"Begin now?" Dan asked.

"There's nothing I'd like more."

3 You Just Can't Get Good Help

Vocabulary

make a mark on something (fixed phrase) when you spill wine on your jeans, you spoil or damage them a little.

priceless (adj) an object so valuable that no price can be given. This is very different from *worthless*.

straight (adj) not gay, in this context. Also a noun meaning a hetero-sexual. The verb, *to straighten* also occurs later in this story.

fuss (n) noise and confusion. When people **make a fuss** (delexical vb) they act more angrily than the situation deserves.

camp (adj) when a man behaves and dresses in a way that some peo-ple think is typical of gay people.

spank (vb) to hit a child with the hand, usually several times on the arse as a punishment.

pile (n) objects positioned one on top of another form a pile, e.g. books, papers, bricks.

fascinate (vb) means to be very, very interested in someone or some-thing. In this context, Casey is referring to an old joke: Work fasci-nates me – I could watch it for hours. *Work fascinates me* should mean that I find my work very, very interesting.

gesture (v) to use hands, arms etc. to express an idea or feeling, in-stead of speaking.

nod (vb) a downward gesture of the head to show that you agree.

dilemma (n) a situation in which it is difficult to choose between two different things that you could do. Or if two people fascinate you at the same time, and you have to make decision.

Casey led Dan into the kitchen. He opened the corner cupboard and took out a mop and bucket, some detergents and rags, a dustpan and brush. He had seen his mother and sister clean once or twice, so he tried things like wiping the refrigerator and microwave doors with the mop, cleaning the oven with the dustpan and brush, polishing the drawer handles. Dan liked new experiences, and cleaning Casey's kitchen was a new experience, but he didn't feel he needed to do it again. It would only be a new experience once. When he finished, he looked around at the fruits of his labour and wondered why he had spent half an hour cleaning something that wasn't dirty when he had started.

When he went back to the living room, Casey was sitting at the table talking on his mobile and making notes. He looked down at Dan's wet feet. "Hang on, honey," he said to the phone. "Go and dry your feet, you idiot. Look at the marks you are making on my priceless Chinese carpet. Fucking straights!" Dan looked around to see what all the fuss was about.

"I zorry," he said.

Casey pointed to the vacuum cleaner and returned to his telephone call. "You just can't get good help these days," laughed at his own campness, and continued, "Oh I know. And a hard man is good to find, don't forget."

When Dan turned the vacuum on, Casey shouted across the room, "You're going to get a good spanking, young man," and laughed again. He marched over to the machine and turned it off. "Here, take these," handing Dan a neat pile of bedclothes. Dan went into the bedroom and changed the sheets while Casey stood at the door, talking on the phone and admiring the human form at work. "Work fascinates me...," he began, and laughed into the phone again. "Oh, you've heard that one too, have you?"

As soon as Dan had finished, Casey lay down on the bed. "Can I go?" asked Dan.

"Go? We've only just begun."

"But school now," he said, pointing to an imaginary watch. Casey gave him three Euro. "You'd better get changed then," Casey said, pointing at the clothes Dan had arrived in. Dan watched Casey's eyes as he took off the now-smelly shorts. Casey smiled and gestured for him to turn around. "And take off the T-shirt too. Turn around. And around." Dan found this game ridiculous, but played along, smiling like a fool. Finally, he bent down to pick up his jeans and flashed Casey another eyeful. When he was dressed, Casey showed him to the door and gave him 10 Euros.

"Very much!" said Dan, happy to have earned so much money for so little effort. He knew that Ivana earned ten Euro for three hours work.

"Yes, and if you'd like to earn some more, you could assist me at my dinner party tonight."

"No. Zorry. Tonight is birthday of grandmother of Ivana."

"Thirty Euro?" Casey offered.

Dan held up three fingers and Casey nodded. What a dilemma. "Time?"

"Come at six."

"*Goot.* I come at six."

"And wear some nice clothes, too. And clean your shoes," he said, miming the action. Dan nodded and left. He had been quite happy being a poor student. A few nice classmates, university, courses, city cafes, Ivana and her mum. Now he felt terrible.

4 The Dinner Party

Vocabulary

I can't be arsed (fixed phrase) To have no motivation to do something. Quite common but not very polite.

launch into (phrasal verb) start something dramatically e.g. a relationship, a speech.

pissed off (adj) to be really annoyed or angry with someone. Derived from the phrasal verb, *to piss someone off*. I can't begin to tell you how pissed off I was!

brand spanking new (fixed phrase) describes something which is very new and impressive.

flood of words (fixed phrase) a lot of words spoken quickly.

casting couch (compound noun) one way of getting a part in a film or play is to have sex with the director.

scold (vb) express your anger with someone by telling them what you think about them.

goatee (n) a beard that is just around the chin.

poke your tongue out (fixed phrase) put your tongue a little way out of your mouth, a rude or a fun sign.

striptease (n) the act of removing your clothing to excite someone. This typically happens as a performance in a strip club.

The doorbell rang. Casey rushed across the living room, ready to launch into his "you're very late" speech. He opened the door saying, "About fucking time!", only to see not one, but two of his ex-lovers standing there smiling. Garry was carrying a couple of bottles of wine, and Dominic made a grand gesture with a huge bunch of sunflowers.

"You're not looking very fabby, Case," said Garry as the host was saying, "Oh shit, it's you.".

"I recognise that am-I-ever-pissed-off face," Dominic says, speaking from bitter experience.

"Come in."

"Are you sure? If we've come at a bad time, we can always go to that brand spanking new KFC down by the station."

"No, no, no. Come in. Leave your shoes on. I can't be arsed."

"Are we early? What's wrong?"

Casey took the bottles of wine that Garry was offering. Just then, the doorbell rang again.

"I hope that's him this time," said Casey, giving the bottles back to Garry.

"A new him?"

Casey rushed back across the living room, ready to launch into his "you're very late" speech. He opened the door to see those soft blue eyes looking into his and his anger suddenly disappeared. "You're very late, young man," he started sternly. "Some dinner guests have already arrived and they've had to hang their jackets themselves." Casey couldn't quite believe he had said that and was glad that Dan couldn't understand his flood of words. So was Dan. He could see that Casey's angry tone didn't match the soft expression in his face. Casey introduced the guests and they had to correct him. "My! You are in a tizz! Actually I'm Garry, ..."

"and I'm Dominic. Have I got a role for you."

"Put a sock in it, Dominic," said Garry, embarrassed but glad that Dan couldn't understand.

"I don't think that'll be necessary!" replied Dominic without taking his eyes off Dan's crotch.

"This is not a casting couch." Garry turned to Dan and said, grading his language like a good English teacher, "Hello Dan, I don't believe I've had the pleasure," as he looked him up and down.

"And I don't believe you will," said Dominic as he arranged the sunflowers in a tall vase.

"You were supposed to wear some nice clothes," scolded Casey. "Come here." Dan followed him into the bedroom, where Casey handed him a white shirt and a jacket. He changed and returned to the living room looking like an advertisement for men's cologne. When the guests saw him, their eyes widened and they took a deep collective breath, as if they were smelling that cologne. My, oh my! Queer eyes for the straight guy, indeed!

The doorbell rang. Casey waved at Dan to open the door. As he did, Andreas, their Austrian friend, a man about Casey's age with a salt and pepper goatee, said, "Ich habe die ganze Welt bereist und du warst die ganze Zeit hier!" (*I travelled the whole world and all this time you were here.*)

"Haben Sie mich lange gesucht?" answered Dan. (*Were you looking for me for a long time?*)

Andreas turned red. The others laughed as Dan showed him in. He handed Dan a big white box containing dessert, and looked at the others. "Why didn't someone warn me he spoke German?"

Dominic said, "I didn't know he spoke anything. He's the quietest little thing Case has ever had here."

"We thought he might have been a deaf mute – you know, one of Casey's typical charity cases."

Casey half-poked his tongue out and turned away to put on some music that he was sure none of them could have heard before. He hoped that they would never forgive him for keeping this great new music from them until now. The only one among them who had heard the Scissor Sisters was Dan. When the music began, he remembered his striptease and had to stop himself from moving in time to the music.

Dan was instructed to set the table and bring out serving dishes. The guests were called to the table and the lights were dimmed.

5 Ah! Those Czech Boys

Vocabulary

ex-pat (n) a person who lives in a foreign country and does not integrate into their new country. Ex-pats typically socialise together, often not learning much of the local language.

is to die for (adj) excellent or extremely desirable.

shriek (n) a short, loud, high cry, especially one produced suddenly as an expression of a powerful emotion. "Real men" do not shriek.

homage (unc. noun) deep respect and often praise shown for a person or god. Dominic has a different "god".

mouth-watering – see salivate in Notes on p.19.

scoff (vb) laugh and speak about a person or idea in a way which shows that you think he or it is stupid or ridiculous. Rhymes with *cough*.

size queen (compound noun) someone who likes large penises

follow it up (phrasal verb) find out more about something, or take further action connected with something.

sex maniac (compound noun) informally used for someone who not only thinks about sex all the time, but gets as much sex as possible.

be smitten (verb phrase) suddenly fall in love with something or someone. Usually a temporary, short term, strong feeling.

quintet (n) a group of five people who play musical instruments or sing as a group.

Notes

You can take the boy out of the country, but you can't take the country out of the boy is an expression meaning that a person who grows up in a small town can never become an educated, cultured city person.

Der Rosenkavalier (1911) is one of the world's most popular romantic operas. The *Marschallin*, a princess sung by a soprano, falls in love with a boy, *Octavian*. He is sung by a mezzo-soprano – a female singer who dresses and acts as a boy in this role. The opera ends with a **trio** of three female voices: the love triangle of the Marschallin, Octavian and his new girlfriend, Sophie. It is one of the most loved moments in all music.

Tadzio is the beautiful teenager in *Death in Venice* (1912), a novella by Thomas Mann. The Visconti film (1971) stars Dirk Bogarde as Aschenbach, a novelist whose obsession with Beauty costs him his life.

"Oooh, what's that lovely smell?" asked Dominic.

"Dan," said Andreas breathily. Hearing his name, Dan looked up and Andreas smiled into his eyes.

"Andreas, fuck you! We are relying on your common tongue. You're the only one here who can talk to him."

"I don't think that is what Andreas most wants to do with his common tongue," Dominic suggested, as if diplomatically.

"Just explain to the boy how to serve, would you?"

"With his tongue?" asked Andreas.

"Isn't that a bit risky?" asked Garry.

Casey turned to him. "Of course, you wouldn't know about table service, would you, Gazza. You can take the boy out of the country..." Garry curled his lip, hating Casey for using the name Gazza. Dominic understood what Casey was doing and squeezed Garry's hand in support.

Andreas saved the day with, "Yes, I'll train him to be my servant, with pleasure."

"And pain," added Dominic.

Andreas turned to Dan and told him that he should stand nearby and watch to see what people needed – pass the vegetables and condiments around, fetch things from the kitchen, and keep topping up the glasses.

As good ex-pats, they could always find new things to bitch about in Brno, standards of service being their favourite – though not tonight, of course! They chatted about boyfriends, past, present and future, about favourite websites, wikis and blogs, and about favourite songs, singers and films. This led to Dominic's latest little film starring some mouth-watering, young Czech guys. "Nothing to compare with the new *Rosenkavalier* film," said Casey.

They all agreed that the new film was to die for. They were shocked and delighted by the director's decision to cast a beautiful teenage boy to mime the role of Octavian, the beautiful young Count who has an affair with the Marschallin, a much older woman. Casey declared it "a stroke of fucking genius."

"Octavian, the new Tadzio!" shrieked Dominic. "I think I'll call my new film *Octavian's Octave* in homage to his eight inches!"

"How camp!" Casey scoffed.

"Did you say *camp*? What century are you living in?" Garry enjoyed a little revenge.

"What mean eight inches?" Dan interrupted.

"Twenty centimetres," replied the whole table in chorus, making the same gesture. Dan was shocked to think that a penis could be so long.

"Oh, just ignore these size queens," Andreas said. "Du sollst mein Octavian sein." (*You can be my Octavian*).

"Bitte, meine Marschallin?" Dan asked, knowing that Andreas would be surprised that he knew enough about this opera to refer to Andreas as the Marschallin. Dan continued refilling the wine glasses that refused to stay half empty, let alone half full.

"Cheers." Andreas was indeed surprised that Dan had understood the reference, but decided to follow it up later. Garry asked Casey to explain how he had met Dan in the first place. Casey was more than happy to word paint the dimples in Dan's arse cheeks as he fucked the cleaner. Everyone was very surprised and tutted at Dan, smiling in amusement and shaking their heads in mock disapproval.

"You little sex maniac," Dominic said without looking directly at him. "Maybe you'd like to make some real money. How about starring in a little film for me? It's better paid than cleaning."

"Or why don't you film him cleaning?" Casey suggests. "Then we could both pay him! He could lick me clean. That has potential."

"As I remember, you weren't very fond of the camera, Mr How-Many-Centimetres?" Dominic said. In fact, Casey had thrown Dominic out of an otherwise promising relationship when he had come across himself on X-Tube. Dominic had secretly filmed him!

After the main course, Dan cleared the table and served coffee and Andreas's very rich dessert. This was followed by a dessert wine and a grand cheese plate. Dan watched in amazement at the volume of food and drink they consumed, and wondered how they could all look so fit. He asked if anyone wanted a cocktail.

Garry answered, "Just half."

Dominic responded, "The first half, I presume?"

"I'll take the second half," Andreas jumped in.

"Aren't you boys just the greediest little things?" Casey said, then wondered why he had even bothered to join in their stupid game.

Dominic and Garry knew the routine. They left the table and moved to the sofa carrying their drinks. When the others followed, Casey changed the music, dimmed the lights and lit some candles. He then instructed Dan to change into a T-shirt before stacking the dishwasher.

"How can you make such a precious thing work like this?" asked Andreas.

"I suppose you'd just pay him to stand around looking pretty," Garry said to Andreas.

"He'd have to do a little more than that," commented Dominic.

Casey explained that as a student, the boy needed the money. Andreas replied that as a student, so did his girlfriend. "Why isn't she here?"

"Well, I can arrange that if you wish. But the boy is quite decorative, don't you think?"

"No, I think he is a gift to the planet and we shouldn't exploit his beauty like this," Andreas said royally.

"You don't suppose Andreas could be a little smitten, do you?" asked Garry.

When Dan had finished in the kitchen, Casey told him to put the jacket and tie back on, but without any shirt. Dan repeated these instructions in German to check with Andreas that he had understood. Andreas nodded and Dan's eyebrows hit his hairline.

When he emerged in the new outfit, the guests were speechless. "Exploit the beauty," Dominic said breathily, breaking the silence.

"The beauty offends me. How dare you be so beautiful?" Casey demanded to know. Everybody's eyes shifted from Dan to Casey as they interpreted this question for themselves – if it was a question.

Garry and Dominic, who were sitting on the couch, immediately moved apart to make room for Dan. Oh, that smell. Casey gave him a glass and Andreas eagerly filled it. They were all fascinated by Dan's life story, which Andreas busily translated from German. *If only these lazy ex-pats would learn some Czech*, Dan thought. With his third glass almost drunk, he had almost stopped noticing Garry's leg brushing against him on one side, and Dominic's on the other side. Garry reached behind Dan to stroke Dominic's fingers.

The candles were going out one by one. The music stopped and the conversation dried up. Andreas broke the silence saying in two languages that he felt hot and was going to take his jacket off. He suggested that Dan do the same. Dominic and Garry helped him remove it.

"It looks like the last act trio is turning into a quintet," Casey said quietly.

"A sextet, if we're lucky," whispered Dominic.

6 A Day at the Beach

Vocabulary

lotion (n) a thick liquid that you or someone else puts on your skin to protect it or to help it get better.

nipples (n) two small dark points on your chest. You probably sucked mother's milk from them many years ago. When erect, you can see the pointy tips in T-shirts.

to **turn** a person **on** (phrasal vb) means that they feel sexually excited because of you – you don't have to do anything. This is different from turning a light on.

pinch (vb) squeeze strongly and quickly between your finger and thumb. It usually causes a short, sharp pain.

taint (n) on a man, the area between the balls (or scrotum) and the arse crack.

blackmail (vb) If you don't pay me a million dollars, I will tell the newspapers that you … This is blackmailing someone.

tension (u.n.) the degree to which something is stretched, physically or emotionally.

interrupt (vb) stop a person from speaking for a short period by saying or doing something.

terrace(n) a flat area outside a building, often with a stone floor, table and chair, glass of wine, Caesar salad, etc.

naughty (adj) bad behaviour of children. A naughty adult is either behaving like a child or it is lightly sexual.

Notes

pull someone's leg (idiom) means to joke with someone, say something that is not quite true. It can have a sexual meaning too. To pull yourself or someone can mean to masturbate. And it is not difficult to imagine that a penis can be referred to as a leg, a third leg, etc.

salivate (vb) Pavlov's dog is the world's most famous "salivater": it was "trained" to produce a liquid (saliva) in its mouth when he (or she?) heard a bell. A wet mouth helps us prepare food for digestion. We say that something or someone is **mouth-watering**. When you *salivate over someone*, you have a strong sexual desire for them. Colloquial: *drool over* someone. You might drool when you are *smitten* with someone.

Ivana was sitting on Dan's crotch massaging suntan lotion into his chest. She was surprised to find his nipples so sensitive today – touching them had never turned him on much before. The passers-by and beach sitters could not see that every time she pinched them, his bathing costume reacted against her own. Eventually, the pressure was too much, and he really had to turn over. She massaged the lotion into his back and then his legs. Her fingertips poked his taint just often enough to cause him to, well, almost … And then his phone rang.

He begged her to stop and pass him the phone. "Only if you turn over," she blackmailed him, so that she could see the tension both in his face and in his Speedos. She got her wish and he got his. When Dan saw the name on the phone display, he spoke in German. She relaxed back into his crotch and teased his nipples.

"Hi!"

"Ahh, my little Octavian. Hi!" Andreas and Dan chatted away in German. "Are you still right for tonight? *Tosca*, remember?"

"Oh hell. Is that tonight? I didn't realise." Ivana was still rubbing suntan lotion into him and he was finding it difficult to breathe normally.

"Are you OK?" Andreas asked. "Where are you?"

"We're at the lake." He smiled at Ivana and she pinched both his nipples. He tried to push her fingers away but she pinched him even harder and he screamed.

"Are you sure you're OK?"

"Ivana seems to have discovered my nipples. I don't know where she found about these little hot spots, but she learns too fast."

"Well, sorry if I'm interrupting."

"You're not. She must have noticed the attention I've started paying to them myself."

"Well, you only have yourself to blame. Anyway, for your info, I'm lying on the terrace where none of the neighbours can see me."

"Can you see them?"

"No, but I can see the castle. What's it called?"

"Spilberk."

"Named after Steven Spielberg, I presume. Did he make a film in it?"

"Yes, *Heart of Darkness*. Have you seen it?"

"You're pulling my leg."

"I'm sure you don't need my help. What else can you see? The cathedral, I guess."

"Yes, what's it called?"

"Pavlov!"

"Oh, so when the church bells ring, every man and his dog starts salivating. Is that right?"

"Ha ha. Sorry, it's Petrov, not Pavlov. It's the Cathedral of Saints Peter and Paul." Dan changed the subject. "What are you wearing?"

"Less than you!" Dan smiled at this answer, still looking at Ivana. She pressed herself hard into Dan's crotch.

"You alone?"

"No."

"Who are you with?"

"You, of course. I'm using both hands," Andreas boasted.

Dan stopped breathing and then cried out like Tarzan. Ivana shook her finger at the naughty little boy. Andreas laughed into the phone. "That was great. *Tosca*. See you at the theatre at 7.00. Dress nicely."

7 A Night at the Opera

Vocabulary

wank (vb) British slang for masturbate, a.k.a. jerk off, pull yourself, beat off, rub one out, self-abuse, have sex with someone you love, toss yourself off, whack off (and a few hundred other less likely expressions).

a closeted person (coll.) does not tell anyone about their sexual orientation. You can also be a closet drinker, a closet Madonna fan, a closet opera lover, etc.

status (u.n.) an official position especially in a social group: high status, low status.

champus (u.n.) champagne

shattered (adj) break suddenly into very small pieces, especially glass. Metaphorically, your heart can be shattered.

toast (vb) when you hold up your glass and then drink to show good wishes.

spare (adj) you should have a spare tyre in the boot of your car, an extra one.

treat (vb) behave towards someone or something in a particular way: treat someone well, treat someone with respect, treat opera as …

respectively (adv) in the same order as the items that you have just mentioned, e.g. *Elizabeth and Barrack are queen and president respectively.*

swap (vb) give something and be given something else instead. I'll swap you my X for your Y.

"Oh, look! There's Andreas, honey!" Dominic took his hand from Garry's arm and waved. Andreas greeted them with his usual charm, but was suddenly stressed: "Have you seen *him* yet?"

"Hope you aren't expecting Case tonight," Garry said.

"He's totally given up culture, he claims," Dominic said.

"You can't give up culture any more than you can give up eating …" Andreas scoffed.

"… or drinking," added Dominic.

"… or wanking," they all said together and laughed.

"No, actually I'm waiting for *him* with a capital D," explained Andreas.

"You're not bringing that boy to the opera, are you?"

"He loves it, apparently. Grew up with it. His dad's a bit of a singer. But since moving to Brno to study, he's had to hide it from his friends."

"Oh, the poor boy. So closeted!" Dominic exclaimed.

"It's just so horrible being in a minority, always having to pretend," Garry said.

"So you can see how lucky he is to have found me," Andreas said, laughing at his status as hero, martyr and saviour.

"Let's go upstairs and I'll get us all a little champus before curtain up," said Garry.

"Be a honey and get an extra one," said Andreas through a warm little smile.

As Garry returned with a tray and was handing Andreas and Dominic their champagnes, he whispered, "Don't look now!" This was clearly a signal for them to turn and almost break their necks. Dan floated across the room like a handsome Teutonic knight arriving on the back of a swan. He was dressed in a fine copy of an Armani suit, his thick hair tied back loosely. His perfect teeth and perfect smile almost blinded them. And those eyes! When Andreas's glass slipped from his fingers and shattered into a million pieces, the foyer fell silent. Even more eyes followed Dan as he floated over to Andreas & co. Dominic handed Dan the fourth glass. Just when they had all toasted and Andreas had started to apologise for his stupidity, Casey appeared out of nowhere. The temperature dropped.

"We heard you'd given up culture," Garry attempted to fill the silence.

"Nonsense! And what's he doing here, may I ask?"

"No, you may not," Andreas replied. Dan tried to relax and look comfortable, but he could not look Casey in the eye. The situation became even more awkward when Ivana turned up and rested her hand on Casey's arm.

"What are you doing here?" Dan asked her in Czech. She told him that Casey had rung her an hour ago to say he couldn't find anyone else wanting a ticket tonight. Although opera was not her thing, she hoped that accepting it might lead to getting her job back.

Ivana was just as curious. "And what are you doing here? I didn't know you liked opera."

"I love it, actually. I grew up with Mozart, Verdi, and Puccini on Dad's old record player. And when Andreas rang me with a ticket, well, I've never actually seen an opera live on stage."

"Who is Andreas? When did he ring you? Why didn't you tell me you were going to the opera? And why did you treat this great love of opera as some dark secret? I wonder what other secrets you have."

Before Dan could answer her, Andreas rested his hand on the young man's arm. Casey did the same to Ivana. At the same time, Andreas and Casey said to Dan and Ivana in German and English respectively, "Time to go in."

Ivana asked Casey if they could swap tickets so that she could sit with Dan. Casey looked at Andreas, then at Dan. Andreas looked at Casey, then at Dan. Then together, Andreas and Casey said "No. Sorry. Out of the question." Everyone laughed without really knowing why, and they all went into the theatre.

8 Ivana Starts Teaching Dan English

"Open the book to page 47. What is on the page?"

"A picture."

"Is it a photo, a drawing, or a painting?"

"Photo."

"Good. A photo. What was my question?"

"There is a painting or photo?"

"No. Start with the verb."

"Is there a photo?"

"That's better. But there were three things."

"Is there a photo, a painting, a ... What was other?"

"What was *the other thing*?" she corrects him. "A drawing."

"Is there a photo, a drawing, or a painting?"

"OK. Tell me five things you can see in the photo."

"Two men."

"Yes, *there are* two men."

"There are furniture."

"Furniture is uncountable..."

"There is furniture."

"Good. There is some furniture. Can you name the items?"

"Bed. There is a bed. There is a chair. There is a ... something with mirror."

"Wardrobe."

"Wardrobe with mirror. Through mirror we see a little woman."

"There is *a* wardrobe with *a* mirror. Good. And we can see a small woman *in* the mirror. Repeat after me." Ivana said each phrase and Dan repeated it.

"Anything else?"

"There is a coat on the mirror."

"Good. It's *hanging* on..."

"There is a coat hanging on the mirror. And a tree. And fireplace."

"And there is a *plant* and *a* fireplace."

"It is very luxury."

"It looks very *luxurious*. Like Casey's flat?"

"No much."

"*Not* much. Describe one of the men in the picture."

"He lies on bed. Maybe sleeping. Has only swimmers."

"He is lying on the bed. He might be sleeping. He is wearing only swimmers."

"He is about 30. Beautiful."

"Do you think he is beautiful?"

"Very sexy. Maybe model."

"Do you think he is sexy?

"Yes. He lies on bed very sexy."

"He *is lying* on the bed very *sexily*," she said, a little annoyed.

"Think you too?"

"Don't you think so?"

"You said questions start with verbs."

"That is for auxiliary verbs and modals. With full verbs, you need to use some form of *do*. What are the auxiliary verbs?"

"*Be* and *have* and *do*."

"And what are the modals?"

"Can, could, will, would, shall, should, may, might, and must."

"Very good. So *think* is a full verb. When you make a question with a full verb, you need to use some form of *do* at the beginning, then the subject, then the verb. For example, I think the other man is his brother. Make a question."

"No, he is not."

"You have to ask me that question. *Do you …*"

"Do you think other man his brother?"

"Not bad. Do you think *the* other man *is* his brother?"

"No. It is same man at different time. Before lie down."

"Do you think the other man is the same man at a different time? Before he lay down?"

"No. But it's possible."

"Tell me about the other man."

"He stands."

"He *is standing*. Use *ing* forms."

"The other man is standing. He is wearing swimmers too. Only swimmers. He looks at sleeping man."

"Good. He *is looking* at the sleeping man. Is he sexy, too?"

"He looks like sleeping man, so he is beautiful and very sexy, too."

"Maybe they are going to have sex."

"That can be amazing."

"That *would be* amazing."

"That would be amazing. Two beautiful men have sex."

"Use the *ing* form."

"Two beautiful men having beautiful sex. Together."

"How can that be beautiful? Two men!"

"Don't questions start with verbs?"

"Not if they start with *wh* words. For example ...?"

"Who, what, where, when, why, which, and how."

"Very good. What was my question?"

"How can that be beautiful?"

"Yes. Two men! You mean like Casey?"

"Casey is only one man."

"But he has sex with men. Do you think that that is OK?"

"Of course. You see magazines in flat. Artistic, no?"

"Yes, I saw the magazines in his flat. And yes, they were good photos. But the idea of two men in love, well, doesn't that bother you?"

"Not at all. Sex and love not the same. Anyway, one my teachers at school loved me."

"You had sex with a teacher?"

"Verb first?"

"No. I am shocked, so I making a statement. But ... did you have sex with a teacher?"

"No, but I knew his eyes always watch me in special way. Other little things, too."

"Like what?"

"He is PE teacher. He took a shower and looked my body all over. Hungry eyes. Can I say hungry eyes?"

"I'm not sure, but I understand. Too well. That is disgusting. Horrible. Terrible."

"No it not. He has beautiful body and always very nice to me. He make me sexy too. It was a fun."

"Dan. I don't want to talk about this any more. It is not a nice topic. Who is the woman we can see in the mirror?"

"She help at home. Clean."

"Is she a cleaner?"

"Yes, a cleaner."

"How do you know?"

"She wears for cleaning."

"She *is dressed* for cleaning. Like me at Casey's."

"She wears clothes. Sorry, *is wearing* clothes. You is *akt*."

"Very funny. *Akt* is a German word. I was *naked*. Is the cleaner wearing a uniform?"

"Maybe. The swimmers are."

"Are what?"

"Wearing uniform."

"What is she doing?"

"She is looking at standing man through, sorry *in*, the mirror and he looks at her too."

"They *are looking* at *each other* in the mirror."

"Standing man waiting that she go away."

"You wait *for* someone to do something. He *is waiting for her* to go away."

"And then he will go to his boyfriend."

"What? In the teacher's book it said that they are Olympic swimmers. They can't be boyfriends."

"Why not?"

"Olympic swimmers aren't like that."

"Anyone can be 'like that'."

"Even you? Even me?"

"Is possible."

"*It* is possible."

"So you agree."

"Dan, what are you saying?"

"Funny picture. In true, I was fucking the cleaner, and the boss find us like so."

"Yes, very funny. I had not thought of it like that. Casey caught us in the act."

"*Akt* is a German word. Do you mean naked?"

"No, we were *caught in the act*. He saw us doing something we shouldn't have been doing."

"And here the cleaner catches them before the act."

"Rubbish. Nonsense. They are not going to do that. Anyway, I would like my job back."

"Did you ask Casey?"

"Yes, at the opera. But he said he's found someone else."

"He is very fast."

"I was surprised when he said 'he'."

"Maybe a student? All students need money."

"But boys cannot do housework. That is why Casey needs a female cleaner. He doesn't have any women in his life."

"Not even a cleaner!"

"Maybe he knows someone else who needs a cleaner. I could work for someone else."

"But you are a bad girl. You take boyfriend into flat. Fuck in his bed. He cannot say to another man that you are good."

"Do you think it is my fault?"

"Of course. You know it was wrong."

"Dan. You're making me angry."

"What can I say?"

"I just want your support."

"I support. But Casey can stop your work if he not like it. In picture, men live in flat together. They can fuck any time. But in Casey's flat, I can't be there."

"If you like the idea of these men fucking so much, why don't you go and clean for Casey?"

"Is good idea."

9 Having Domestics

Vocabulary

domestic is an adjective that means to do with the house or home. *He's not very domestic*, means his house is usually untidy, messy. Domestic is also a noun – it is a job. Your *domestic* is the person who cleans your house. But the verb phrase, *to have a domestic* refers to a couple arguing or fighting about something.

squirm (vb) move from side to side in an awkward way because you are nervous, embarrassed or in pain.

duel (n) difficult competition in which both sides show a lot of effort. Imagine two 19th century gentlemen on a winters morning, turning to shoot each other with pistols.

get rid of (vb) remove or throw away something you don't want. And you can get rid of a person by having no contact with them.

considerate (adj) a considerate person is kind because they think about (consider) your needs.

sigh (vb) breathe out slowly and noisily, expressing tiredness, sadness, pleasure, boredom.

say something **innocently** (adv.) pretending to not know about something which has made someone sad or angry, for example.

get off on someone (phrasal vb) have an orgasm while having nice thoughts about someone.

Spare me! an exclamation when something unbelievable or otherwise unpleasant has occurred.

lust (u.n.) strong sexual feeling without much emotion. Sometimes used in *to be in lust with someone* playing with the standard phrase, *to be in love with someone.*

Garry was sitting on Dominic's butt and massaging his back, gradually moving downwards. He slid down Dominic's legs a bit and massaged into the dimples of his arse cheeks. Dominic loved that. So did Garry. Garry squeezed some more cream into his hands and sent his middle finger into Dominic. He moaned softly. Garry was working quite slowly, letting Dominic get used to it – which never took long. With his other hand, Garry continued massaging Dominic's lower back. He removed the finger and then sent two in. Dominic squirmed a bit and whispered, "Not yet." He turned over and Garry leaned down to kiss him. Their erections slid around together with the aid of some of the massage cream. Some of the natural cream their cocks produced also helped. Their tongues duelled.

"I wonder if Casey knows how grateful we are," Garry wonders.

"Casey doesn't do gratitude, honey."

"Yes, I suppose he only wanted to get rid of his little Yorkshireman. Honestly, he treated me like some exotic tribesmen. Passed me on to someone else so he wouldn't feel guilty or something."

"Casey doesn't do guilt, either, honey." Dominic drew his finger down the length of Garry's nose and then ran it around his lips. Garry licked it.

"Well, it was very considerate of him, at least. Look at us," said Garry, smiling.

"I don't think he even does considerate!" Garry sat up and tried to wrap one hand around both their duelling cocks. He stretched his other hand across Dominic's chest so he could press into both his nipples.

"And now he's sent me Dan. Turned up in my English class this afternoon. Sitting there in those torn jeans, that tight white T-shirt with his nipples almost poking through it, that hair, those eyes," Garry sighed.

"Hello there?" warned Dominic, as Garry continued to masturbate them.

"The moment he walked into the room, every head turned."

"I hope you didn't drop your champagne."

"Then he sits at his desk, legs spread wide, and rests one hand in his crotch. Looks like he's got a bit to play with down there."

"Are we having a threesome?" Dominic asked threateningly.

"I don't think so," said Garry, obviously distracted by images of Dan. Dominic's cock started to lose interest as Garry's approached the end. As he creamed all over Dominic's chest, neck, and chin, he screamed, "Daaaaaaaaaaa …ooooommmmmmmm … minic."

"Get off me," shouted Dominic, pushing Garry away. Garry started to massage his cream into Dominic's chest, but Dominic grabbed his T-shirt and wiped himself clean. Garry pushed him down onto his back, holding him there and heading for Dominic's now flaccid member.

"Get away from me, you bastard."

"What's the problem, honey?" Garry asked innocently.

"I'm not Dan," Dominic said, almost shouting. "That seems to be the problem. Let me up," he demanded.

"I'm not letting you up until I get you up. What are you talking about?"

"I was having sex with you and you were getting off on Dan. I find that a little bit of a turn off. Sorry."

Garry felt absolutely terrible. Dominic was right. "That's not true!" he whispered forcefully. "I could never do that to you."

"That's bullshit and you know it."

"I love you, Dominic, and you know it."

"Spare me! We've never ever used that word. Don't start now." Garry wanted to look into his eyes but Dominic looked away. "And to use the L word, when you've just got off on Dan, is a joke."

"This is all Casey's fault."

"That's bullshit, and you know it. For all his faults, at least he's honest. Your turn."

"I've never been dishonest with you."

"Until now. And you can just forget Dan. He's got a girlfriend as well as Casey and Andreas fantasizing about him day and night."

"What are you talking about? I don't want a relationship with a straight university student who can't even speak English."

"Not even with that hair, those eyes, and that something down there to play with?"

"Look darling, he's very cute, very sexy, and perfectly delightful."

"Which nobody can deny," Dominic sang.

"But he's not relationship material."

"Just someone to wank over."

"Well, yes, maybe," Garry admitted through a little smile.

"Well, just fuck off then." Dominic fought his way out of Garry's grip and went to the bathroom. Garry fell on the bed and rubbed Dominic's arse smells into the thick dark hair around his cock. He quickly got an erection.

"Dominic, I love you," he whispered as he came again.

When he woke up half an hour later, Dominic was gone. He had left a note saying that he was going to the sauna to find some true lust that didn't pretend to be anything else.

Garry sat on the couch pressing the note to his chest. He had a good cry. A few hours later he rang, but Dominic didn't answer. Garry sent several texts which were not answered.

At around 10:00 p.m., Garry opened a bottle of wine, took out his journal, and started to write about all of the recent events.

10 Thank Your Lucky Stars

Vocabulary

drunk as a skunk (idiom) the animal skunk is not known to be a big drinker. This idiom is based on the rhyme. It simply means the result of drinking too much alcohol.

tablet (count n.) usually round and often white, though Viagra is a tablet which is not round and not white. Tablets are supposed to make you feel better.

vomit (vb) throw up what you've eaten, perhaps because the meat was bad, or because you've had too much to drink.

wretched (adj) looking and feeling very ill or very unhappy. Two syllables.

sob (vb) cry noisily, taking in deep breaths. Here a noun, *a fit of sobs*.

unintelligible (adj) cannot be heard clearly or understood.

loosen (vb) make something less tight often to be more comfortable.

spray (vb) cover someone or something with very small drops of a liquid, e.g. to spray-paint a car, spray someone with water to make them cooler.

When Dominic arrived home in the middle of the night, drunk as a skunk, the first thing he saw was Garry's lifeless body resting peacefully on the kitchen table. There was blood and tablets and broken glass all over the table and floor.

"This can't be happening," Dominic cried. He moved towards the body but before he could touch it, he froze. He looked at each little piece in the scene and tried to connect them into a single logical story. But he couldn't concentrate. He felt for his phone in his pocket but couldn't find it. He ran back to the entrance hall where his jacket was hanging and tried the pockets. He was so drunk. As he looked around, he saw a list of emergency numbers pinned to the back of the door. He'd never noticed them before. "Fuck you, Garry," he said as he started to phone the emergency number. "English, woman, English! *Anglicky*. This is an emergency." The English-speaking operator told him that an ambulance would be there in a few minutes.

He waited and waited. It felt like it would never come. When the doorbell finally rang, he had to run downstairs to let the paramedics in. They looked like a father and son. The younger one explained that they were just finishing their shift and were about to go home when the call came. "Well, I hope I am not spoiling your evening, gentlemen. But someone is dying in my flat."

When they got inside, Dominic showed them the scene. The older man lifted Garry's body, and some sounds came out. It was nothing that anyone could understand, but at least it meant Garry wasn't dead. Dominic thanked his lucky stars. The younger man crouched down to look at the label on the shattered bottle of *Sangue de Toro* and nodded to his colleague. He put his finger into the pool of blood and then licked it. He said to his colleague in Czech, "Quite a nice drop. Though I prefer our Moravian wines myself." The two men smiled.

Dominic's whole body froze in anger as these clowns seemed to be making a joke of a not very funny situation. "Can't you do something? He's still breathing. Didn't you hear that sound he made?"

The younger one held up the label and pointed at the bull painted on it. "This is bull's blood, not your boyfriend's. Let's get him to bed." Dominic now recognised the meaning of the Spanish wine label. The older colleague left them to sort it out.

Dominic tried to make some apologies as he showed the man out. He felt sick from his own drunkenness, the fright of losing Garry, and now this whole embarrassing situation. He went to the bathroom and vomited. As he saw his wretched face in the mirror he burst into a fit of sobs.

The ambulance nurse came in and rested his hands on Dominic's shoulders. "Come on. Everything's OK. He'll be fine." Dominic said something unintelligible through his sobs. "You must love him very much," he continued. Dominic's breathing gradually slowed down. The nurse said, "Now let's get you out of these stinking clothes." Dominic raised his arms like a helpless child and the nurse lifted the T-shirt off him. Then he loosened his belt and Dominic stepped out of his jeans and underwear. The nurse turned the shower on, helped Dominic in, and sprayed him all over.

"I don't know how I can thank you enough," Dominic finally managed to say.

"A blow job would be just fine," the nurse answered quite matter-of-factly. "I'm off duty, now." He dropped his pants and stepped into the shower. Dominic looked down at another fine specimen of Czech manhood.

"I'm sorry, but I'm completely shattered. I can't." After a bit more washing and massaging, Dominic added, "I really do love him, you know," as if he was just realising it.

"Well, you're a very lucky couple. Now turn around." Dominic turned, and the nurse sprayed his back and stuck his soapy finger in Dominic's arse. Dominic offered him a role in his next film, which he would call *Lucky Stars*.

11 Dan Is Offered More Work

Vocabulary

flirt (vb) show that you are sexually attracted to someone in a light-hearted way.

distorted when the shape of something looks unnatural when seen in a funny mirror or through water, for example.

crouch (vb) bend your knees and lower your body so that you are close to the ground and leaning forward slightly. Try it!

splash (vb) when liquids get on your body or clothes. It is usually a bad thing, but you might splash your face with cold water to help you wake up.

I don't know what came over me is a phrase that usually means: I wasn't thinking, I didn't mean to do/say this. It is often part of saying sorry.

mess (n) something or someone that looks dirty or untidy. You can make a mess, clear up or clean up a mess.

rage (u.c.) very strong anger. Some people turn red when they are enraged.

embrace (vb) wrap your arms around someone to show your warm feelings for them.

fun fair (compound noun) a place where you can go on exciting rides and play games to win prizes.

OJ is orange juice. **JO is** jack off, another slang term for masturbation. Here it refers to another juice – semen.

When Dan saw "Andreas" on his phone display, he started speaking German, bringing another English lesson with Ivana to an end. Dan asked Andreas to wait a moment as he said goodbye to her. After she left, they chatted about this and that. When the possibility of cleaning for Andreas came up, he invited Dan over to discuss the details. It was obvious to Dan that Andreas was flirting with him. He didn't mind, and anyway, it was great to have a native speaker to practice German with.

An hour later, Dan arrived at Andreas's flat, a little earlier than they had agreed. He had to ring the doorbell several times before Andreas opened the door. Andreas had nothing on but a dressing gown and Dan could hear the shower still running. As Dan apologised for interrupting his shower, a voice called out in English, "Where are the clean towels?" Dan realised that he had interrupted more than a shower. As Andreas switched to English to answer, Dan looked him up and down and smiled, thinking, *You're not too old for a bit of mid-afternoon recreation.* Dan was sure that in such a situation he would feel embarrassed, but Andreas clearly was not. He invited Dan inside. Dan left his shoes at the door and followed Andreas into the kitchen, where he declined a beer but accepted an orange juice. Andreas asked him to wait in the kitchen while he attended to his visitor.

"He's just leaving," Andreas whispered. As Dan politely smiled and looked into his glass of OJ, he saw the naked visitor's erection distorted in the glass. His eyes opened wide, and he looked up to see the torso and then the face of Dominic. Andreas moved to stand between them but it was too late. Dominic said, "So this is the late afternoon shift coming in, is it?"

Dan did not understand the joke, but he said hello and looked from Dominic to Andreas. "I thought the doorbell was someone selling bibles," said Dominic. Dan looked at the kitchen clock and said that he would come back some other time.

Andreas told Dominic that his time was up, which made Dominic angry. In one movement, he opened Andreas's dressing gown, knelt and took Andreas in his mouth. Andreas was struggling with pleasure and embarrassment. Dan's glass slipped from his fingers and shattered into a million pieces all over the kitchen floor. The juice splashed everyone. Dan apologised and grabbed something to wipe up the juice. He crouched down, coming dangerously close to Dominic's head, which was becoming more and more energetic as his mouth noisily serviced Andreas's cock. Dominic offered Dan a turn, but Dan shook his head and closed his eyes. Andreas begged, "Please, Dan," and then his own juice splashed all over Dominic's chest and Dan's trousers. Andreas told Dan to wipe up that juice, too. Dan shook his head angrily and stood up.

"I'm sorry, I don't know what's come over me," Dominic laughed as he apologised. He looked at his watch and exclaimed that he really had to leave. He marched into the bedroom to get dressed, leaving Dan and Andreas to clean up the OJ and JO messes.

Dan wanted to leave too, but Andreas asked him to stay. After all, he had been invited at this time. Andreas went into the bathroom and had a quick wash. He returned to the living room wearing a caftan. Dan was still shaking with rage at what he had just witnessed. Andreas apologised for Dominic's behaviour and said that he and Garry were having problems. "I was just trying to help," he explained. Dan thought Andreas was just helping himself. There was no way that Andreas was helping either Dominic or Garry. He started to wonder if he wanted Andreas's friendship at all.

Andreas put a CD on and went into the kitchen to make some coffee. Dan refused to admit that he recognised *Der Rosenkavalier*. He looked around at the modern wall lights, the thick colourful rugs spread across the dark wooden floors, the grand bookshelves full of books and CDs and DVDs and magazines and ornaments. There were plants everywhere, a hi-fi, and a large flat-screen TV mounted on the wall.

Dan stroked the leather couch. He lay down on it and pressed his nose into the leather, inhaling deeply. The music filled the room. Dan picked up one of the German magazines from the glass top coffee table. He was not surprised that it was a gay magazine and he would read anything in German. He was surprised, however, that it looked like an intelligent, well-written lifestyle magazine, similar to those his mother and sister read. Fitness and health and holidays and cooking and news from around the world. There were pictures of couples in bars, in warm embraces, and at sporting events and fun fairs, as well as pictures of politicians and priests, famous singers and actors, and all that stuff.

He laid the open magazine across his chest. Andreas floated into the living room gracefully, as if on the back of a swan, and placed a tray on the coffee table. Dan couldn't help admiring the stylish cups and plates, the milk pot and sugar bowl, and the expensive little biscuits. Andreas lit some Japanese incense sticks on the mantelpiece and moved back to the couch. "Everything is so beautiful," Dan said softly. He moved to sit up, but Andreas gently lifted his legs, sat down, and then draped Dan's legs across his lap. "Even ze orchestra is beautiful," Andreas quoted through a soft smile. He rested his arm across Dan's OJ & JO flavoured trousers and gently drew figures of eight on the boy's kneecap.

12 Planning a Trip to Vienna

Vocabulary

sweep (vb) clean a floor by using a brush or a broom to collect the dirt into one place from which it can be removed.

dustpan (n) flat container with a handle into which you brush dust and dirt.

Jeff Stryker an American porn star. Sometimes with dirt on his face and arms, as if in a war zone, etc. See Wikipedia.

blush (vb) when your face turns red, usually from embarrassment. Common among teenagers.

freeze (vb: freeze, froze, frozen) Water freezes at 0 degs Celsius. When a person freezes, it can be from the cold weather, or because they are very surprised and therefore unable to move.

stand to attention (verb phrase) the way soldiers stand, upright especially when an officer is shouting at them.

foreskin (n) loose skin which covers the end of the penis. If you have one, you are uncircumcised, uncut. If you are don't you are or have been circumcised, cut.

flick (vb) a short sudden movement.

go commando not to wear underwear.

Casey sat at his desk in the corner of the living room, typing, pausing, and then typing some more. He occasionally made or answered a phone call. Dan brought a tray from the kitchen and put it in front of Casey. Casey half smiled in gratitude but was too involved in his work and waved him away. Dan went back to the bathroom to continue cleaning it, but instead he spent most of the time tousling his hair in different ways and admiring his face from different angles in the reflections of the reflections. He wondered what advantages his beauty might bring him.

Casey told Dan to set the fire. When Dan removed his T-shirt, the typing stopped and Casey fell into deep thought. Dan knelt beside the fireplace brushing the ash into a dustpan. He took some wood from the neat little pile and built a small pyramid.

"What a mess you are. Covered in Jeff Stryker dirt, you are. That's enough for today. Go and clean yourself up."

"What about bedroom?"

"That'd be nice."

Dan blushed and looked away as he realised that Casey was deliberately misinterpreting his words. Dan went back into the bathroom, stripped off his pants and spent another half a minute in front of the mirror, a little angry at his parents and grandparents and great-grandparents for giving him only an almost perfect face and body. He had a quick shower. When he finished, he realised that he would have to clean the bathtub again. Dan started to wonder what he was doing, working as a house boy for some English fag.

"I brought you an old towel," Casey said to that not unfamiliar arse.

Dan looked around to see what a towel was. "Thank you," he said and returned to the cleaning.

"I thought you'd already cleaned the bathroom." Dan looked at him and raised his eyebrows. Casey could tell he was pissed off. "How did you get your back so messy?" Casey stepped into the bathroom, squeezed some liquid soap into his hand, and massaged it into Dan's back. Dan froze. Casey squeezed some more soap into his hand then onto Dan's back, further down. As he reached Dan's butt, Dan straightened up and Casey could see his cock standing to attention in the mirror. It was much smaller than he had remembered it. It must have been all that loose foreskin.

"What about the bedroom?" Casey asked through a nervous smile.

"Thirty Euro?" Dan asked sarcastically.

"Fuck off, then." Casey washed his hands and flicked the water on Dan's back.

Dan came out of the bathroom with the old towel wrapped around him. "Anything else today?" he asked.

"Yes. We're going to Vienna on Friday, so you'll be organising the train tickets, and finding some accommodation. And do try to get some tickets for the opera."

Dan was a bit shocked – not only the cheap houseboy, but now a personal assistant! He said, "I am dressed like cleaner, not like secretary." The towel dropped to the floor and he put his old trousers on. He certainly liked going commando!

"Don't you want to come to Vienna with me?"

"I thought you and Andreas." Dan lifted his head. His eyes grew wider and he smiled. "I was never in Vienna." He put his T-shirt on.

"You'll love it. They speak German there!"

"Really?" Dan pretended to be surprised. "Why you not say me before? Is very interesting to me."

"You don't want to know. Just try a search for Vienna, accommodation. There'll be plenty for up to 100 Euro per night. Get their numbers and ring them. We are staying Friday and Saturday nights."

"What'll they ask?"

"Haven't you ever booked a hotel?"

"No. I am not ever staying in one, too."

"My dear boy." Casey looked at Dan so long and so hard that he saw right into the young man's soul.

Dan felt Casey's eyes burning into him. "Am I more attractive because I not stay in hotel?"

"Yes, for some reason you are." Casey felt that he was holding a blank book in his hands, and that he was the one who had been given the great honour of writing in it. What a frightening responsibility! And yet, he was sure he could rise to the challenge. He could rise to most challenges. Casey got up from the desk, waved Dan into position in front of the computer and left him to get on with it. Dan had never used the internet for finding information like this, and it took him quite a while to find anything. He made a list.

13 Never-Ending Preparations

Vocabulary

Sklave German word for the English *slave*.

Girl Friday a female helper or office worker who is willing to do all sorts of work.

Pension as used here, is not an English word, rather it is one of those "Euro" words that appears in most European languages except English – like variations on *ananas*, which means pineapple. Pension is a type of tourist accommodation, something like a Bed & Breakfast in Britain.

basement a part of a building below ground level consisting of one or more rooms.

let someone down (phrasal verb) not doing something well disappoints someone. You let them down. They feel let down.

"Could you come here for a moment?" Casey called Dan into the bathroom to wash his back.

"Not just your cleaner and secretary, now I *Sklave* also?"

"And travelling companion, don't forget," Casey added. This was not meant as blackmail. Dan squeezed some liquid soap into his hands and rubbed it into Casey's back as he had recently learnt to do. "Lower, lower, Girl Friday!"

"Enough is enough," Dan said.

"What accommodation have you reserved?"

"Nothing. I made a list. You read it first, then I call some."

"Good idea. Lower, lower."

"Bad idea. Your back is very clean. Shining. That is enough." Dan left the bathroom and decided to ring one of the numbers on his list.

One of the pensions he had found claimed to be gay friendly. It even had a sauna in the basement. Dan was certain that Casey would like it, so he rang to ask if there were any rooms and how much they cost. When the receptionist told him that it was booked out, he felt strangely disappointed. He felt he had somehow failed, that he had let Casey down. Although Dan didn't feel comfortable making expensive international calls, at the same time he wanted to keep the receptionist talking. He asked when there would be a free room on a Friday and Saturday. The receptionist offered to send him an email of available dates. While Dan was giving him his email address, the receptionist interrupted to say that he had just gotten an email cancellation. Dan couldn't believe his luck. When Dan gave Casey's surname for the booking, the receptionist said, "That's not by any chance *Casey* Ravenscroft, is it? Well, why didn't you say so? Casey always has a place here." Dan wondered why Casey hadn't asked him to book this pension in the first place. "So you must be his new boy, are you?"

"I thought I was his cleaner, but he just called me his Girl Friday."

"Well, we all are certainly looking forward to meeting YOU."

Dan asked about breakfast, times of arrival and departure, method of payment, and the need to pay a deposit. He had read all of this information on the internet, but he hoped that asking such questions made him sound like someone with a lot of experience.

When Casey came out of the bathroom, Dan proudly informed him, "I found nice pension near centre." When Casey heard the name, his performance could have won him an Oscar.

"What! You booked us into that place. Fuck. Did you give them my name? Shit, last time I stayed there … you don't want to know. I don't even want to think about it. Maybe it's for the best. Fuck."

"Casey, I have to go now. We go with Ivana to film in evening."

"Who is 'we'?"

"I and Ivana."

"We don't use *we* like that. You put yourself last, too. We say, 'Ivana and I are going to see a film.'"

"Thank you, Mr. Teacher."

"What are you going to see, Girl Friday?

"New film, *Shortbus*."

"Well that should give you a few good ideas." Casey opened his wallet to pay Dan for his work, but Dan refused.

"Thank you, Mr. Casey, but you are paying in *Wien*. I cannot take money."

"Aren't you just the perfect young gentleman? But you will be working in Vienna." Dan was shocked. "Didn't I tell you? You'll be interpreting for me."

"But my English is not so good."

"It is OK for what I need. Your German is the important thing this weekend."

Dan smiled broadly. After years and years of studying German, it was finally being rewarded.

14 All the Way to Vienna

Vocabulary

bump (vb) hit something lightly and accidentally.

ventilation (n) a system of moving fresh air around an enclosed space.

reluctant (adj) not very willing to do something and therefore often slow to do it.

drain water goes down a drain from a bath, toilet, kitchen sink, etc. when it is no longer needed. When your **plans go down the drain** (idiom) you are angry, annoyed, disappointed, frustrated etc. because something has stopped your plan from going ahead.

wink (vb) close and open one eye very quickly. When we *give someone a knowing wink* we show each other that we understand the same thing.

adjust clothes (vb) arrange your clothing to make yourself look better.

stress out (phrasal verb) to make some very worried, nervous.

Casey arrived at the station a full half-hour before departure time and immediately started looking around the overcrowded main hall for Dan. Mid-afternoon Friday is a busy time at railway stations. Casey was repeatedly bumped and knocked by people (sorry) and their big backpacks (sorry), guitar cases (sorry), laptops (sorry), and pets (sorry). He was dressed for the opera. There was no ventilation. He wished they had arranged to meet in the restaurant or on the platform. With only ten minutes left, Dan was still nowhere to be seen and he wasn't answering his mobile. And guess who had the train tickets! With only two minutes to go, Casey hurried to the platform cursing the world (sorry).

The Eurocity train arrived on time and Casey reluctantly climbed aboard the first class carriage. Just as the doors closed, he saw a very angry young Dan standing on the platform. Casey didn't look at him – he couldn't believe that his well-laid plans had already gone down the fucking drain.

The conductor appeared ten minutes later calling for tickets, so Casey took his wallet out. He knew he would have to pay the Supercity supplement as well as a fee for buying the ticket on board. He was about to pay when a hand interrupted the transaction. Dan spoke in Czech to the conductor, who punched the tickets and smiled at them both with a knowing wink as Dan sat down next to Casey.

"How did you get on the train?" Casey asked. "The doors were closing."

"I smiled into the conductor's eyes, and did this." Dan demonstrated how he adjusted his crotch. "You fags are not discreet." Dan is going to call this strategy his *indiscreet crotch adjustment*, ICA for short, but he would have to ask Andreas how to say it in English. Dan smiled, wondering how many doors his ICAs would open for him. "Very cheap," Dan said, pretending to be disappointed.

"Well at least one of us is cheap. You are turning out to be very expensive."

"You look bad. Very hot and nervous." Dan took a couple of refresher towels out of his sad looking backpack and gave them to Casey.

"Where did you get these?"

"Ivana gives me them all the time. Because of …" and his hand gestured in front of his crotch.

Casey suggested the missing word: "Wanking?"

Dan shrugged his shoulders and repeated the word. "Wanking. Regular?"

"Me or you?"

"Is it a regular verb?" Dan asked a little impatiently.

"It's the past tense of *wink*," Casey said, winking at him and wondering if he'd be understood.

"Ah, like think: think, thank, thunk."

"No, you wanker. Drink, drank, drunk." Dan looked at him, not sure what to believe now. "Look, I'm not your fucking English teacher. *Wink* and *wank* are two different verbs, both regular." He opened one of the little refresher towels and wiped it all over his face and neck. "That's better. Thanks a lot …for clearing up the mess you made."

"What mess? I haven't wunk yet," Dan said, thinking, as he often did, how much he'd like to embrace his beloved little cock, here and now.

"Wanked," Casey shouted for all the carriage to hear. "You idiot. But you stressed me out by turning up so late."

"I'm sorry. Ivana want me not to come. She kept wanking me, saying don't come." Casey was slightly amused by the double meaning but couldn't be bothered to explain it.

"So her grandmother had gone out for the afternoon, had she?"

They stopped talking when the Czech and Austrian border police checked their passports. The train stopped at the border, then not again until they got to Südbahnof.

Ten minutes into Austria, Casey received a welcoming SMS from his provider, which reminded him to ask why Dan hadn't answered his phone. "No credit."

"You can earn credit, you know?"

Dan smiled into Casey's eyes and tried a little ICA. Casey swallowed and thought again of his well-laid plans. The boy deserved credit.

15 Ah, the Opera!

Vocabulary

bar fridge (compound noun) a small refrigerator.

en suite (n) a bathroom which is directly connected to a bedroom, not usually a main bathroom. A French word used in English.

spectacle (n) a wonderful, grand public event or show.

courtesan (n) a term for a woman who had sexual relationships with rich or important men in exchange for money. They had a higher high social position than prostitutes. The term is used to refer to past.

let on (phrasal vb) provide information, especially when it's secret.

revealing costume (coll) clothes which show more of the body than is usual or acceptable in certain situations.

drive a wedge between people (idiom) when someone does something that damages the relationship two people or groups of people

euphoric (adj) extreme happiness, sometimes with a feeling of being light-headed.

be frustrated feel annoyed because you cannot achieve what you want, such as expressing yourself in a foreign language.

Note

La Traviata is another of the world's favourite operas. Composed by Verdi in 1853. Violetta is a courtesan. She falls in love with Alfredo, a young nobleman. His father will not allow such a relationship and he convinces her to leave her son. This causes a lot of personal tragedy. Violetta has been sick with *consumption* for a long time. When Alfredo returns, his father watches her die in his son's arms. The end. Can you imagine a situation in which two gay men are not allowed to be together, and …?

Casey was not looking forward to meeting his old friend who worked at Pension Wild. Fortunately, he wasn't there when Casey and Dan checked in, though the receptionist gave them both a knowing little smile when he heard Casey's name. When they stepped into their room, the first thing they noticed was the one double bed. Neither of them commented. They played it cool and thought very different things.

"Nice room," said Dan. He inspected the bar fridge and the en suite. "Better than the room I live in. I hope I find something like, when I move out."

"Are you looking for a new flat?"

"Yes, I stay in room of friend who comes back from semester in Spain. Now I have to leave."

"Why don't you get changed for the opera and we'll go and have a bite to eat."

"Changed?"

"Well, you are not going to the opera like that. Didn't you bring anything to wear? *La* fucking *Traviata*. The Vienna State Opera."

Dan hung his head in shame. He looked at his backpack, then smiled into Casey's eyes and adjusted his crotch. Casey hated him for a moment. With a recently learnt gesture, Dan instructed Casey to turn around. Then he got undressed, took some clothes out of his bag and was dressed in his magnificent suit within moments. Casey enjoyed the spectacle in the mirror.

Casey remarked that they still had plenty of time before the consumptive whore would drive a wedge between a noble father and son. Dan felt that it was the father who drove the wedge between the young nobleman and the beautiful courtesan, but his English was not up to it. They went to dine in a fine restaurant which had menus in a dozen languages. After their soup bowls had been taken away, a large middle-aged man approached their table. Casey stood up unusually formally and they shook hands. Casey introduced Dan and instructed him to speak to the man in German. After they had exchanged a few words, Herr Whatshisname left them to enjoy the rest of their meal. "Tomorrow at four, then," were his departing words, which Dan translated.

"Who is that man? And why he look at me like hatred?" asked Dan. Casey explained that this was the man Dan would have to translate for, but didn't say anything about the nature of the business.

They arrived at the Opera House with plenty of time to wander around the foyer and crowd-watch. Casey delighted in seeing so many male couples, who seemed to equally enjoy admiring him and Dan as a couple. He returned their discreet approving nods with his own. Their discreet nods usually included a discreet look at Dan's crotch. Casey had no intention of letting on that Dan did not have a pistol in his pocket – it was just his mobile phone.

Casey enjoyed the opera, but felt the tenor could have shown a bit more emotion. Madam's costume was a bit too revealing for the late 19th century, the English on the small electronic screens at each seat annoyed him from time to time, and the intervals were too long. Worst of all, Casey found it difficult to concentrate when the boy sitting beside him kept adjusting his crotch. Casey wondered what it would take to convince him to wear underwear.

The performance left Dan in a euphoric mood such as he had never before experienced. His head was exploding with the tragedy of the story, the beauty of the music, the spectacle of the sets and costumes, the size of the stage, the volume of the singers, and the intensity of the sound floating out of the orchestra pit.

He was very frustrated that he couldn't say all this to Casey. He could only repeat wonderful thank you fantastic thank you incredible thank you. Casey was happy that Dan was happy. He wished he could be that happy himself.

16 Two Boys, One Bed

Vocabulary

curse (vb) say something which is not polite and shows that you are very angry.

taut as a drum (fixed phrase) tight or completely stretched like the skin of a drum (taut is pronounced the same as taught).

giggle (vb) a nervous or silly laugh, typical of children.

How could you? A phrase expressing dissatisfaction with something someone has done.

fleeting satisfaction (coll) a good feeling that does not last long.

well-appointed (adj) a place that has good furniture, equipment.

overcast (adj) cloudy and therefore not bright and sunny.

morning glory (compound noun) the erection you wake up with in the mornings, often your own.

get a feel for (verb phrase) get a sense for the quality of something.

After a few drinks they went back to the pension and got ready for bed, as Casey said that they had to be in top form for the big meeting tomorrow. Casey came out of the bathroom after a quick shower and cursed silently as he tripped over Dan's clothes. Fucking teenagers! His towel slipped off but it didn't matter as the young prince was fast asleep, his long dark hair fanned across the pillow. Casey turned off the light and climbed gently into bed so as not to wake him. Who said Casey doesn't do considerate? Casey lay on his side and rested his open palm on the royal torso, as taut as a drum, as warm as a summer beach, as still as a calm sea teeming with life below the surface. Casey let his thumb gently stroke the smooth skin. Dan turned his head towards Casey and smiled and giggled. This gave Casey the feeling that he could continue, so he did. He played with the foreskin on Dan's flaccid little cock. Dan's smile disappeared. Minutes passed which seemed like hours, before his fingers lifted Casey's hand away and he turned to face the other way.

Casey hoped that this was an invitation to massage his arse, and he quickly accepted. Of course, there is nothing unpleasant about such a massage, it's just the problem of what it's leading to, and with whom. After a minute, Dan flipped over and shouted in a whisper, "Stop. Please."

"No, I won't," Casey replied, grabbing Dan's now-hard cock.

Dan dug his fingernails into Casey's wrist. "Casey, I'm sorry, but I can't do this. Please."

"Well you shouldn't have booked a double room."

"I didn't know."

"And you shouldn't be sleeping naked."

"I always sleep naked. And I have no things to wear in the bed."

"And you should stop me immediately, not when you've taken what you want and given me nothing but false hope."

"I'm sorry. It was nice. But you want more. Always more."

"You also always want more and more. And you never give."

"Casey, you are old. What can I give you?"

"Old. Did you say old? You little shit. Old? How could you?" Casey got out of bed and put on some shorts and a T-shirt. Dan was amazed to see Casey's naked body – he didn't know cocks could be so thick and so long. Homage to Octavian, indeed.

"Look, what you want me for? For sex? For boyfriend? For work? You like me at all?"

"I don't know. See you later." And with that, Casey left the room and went down to the basement where he hoped to find at least fleeting satisfaction in the well-appointed sauna.

When Dan woke up the next morning, the sky was overcast. Casey was beside him asleep on his back, with his morning glory doing a pretty good imitation of a skyscraper. It looked even bigger in daylight and Dan couldn't stop himself from having a little look under the sheets. He wrapped his fingers around his own little skyscraper and dragged the foreskin over it. *I don't think my fingers would touch if I tried to wrap them around Casey's cock*, he thought. He wondered if he could get a feel for its size without waking him. He formed a capital C with his thumb and middle finger and surrounded the tower which had starred in Dominic's film. He tried to make his fingers touch, but found that they did not in fact meet. At that very moment, he shot his load into his other hand.

17 A Freudian Slip

Vocabulary

retail therapy (compound noun) going shopping to make yourself feel better, to improve your mood. A modern, ironic expression.

pedestrian area (compound noun) part of town or city where cars cannot go, only people on foot.

horse-drawn (adj) pulled by a horse. Typical inner-city tourist attraction.

protest (vb) say something forcefully or complain about something.

to have a **finger in the pie** (idiom) to be involved in something, have an financial interest in a business.

a domestic an argument between a couple

seduce (vb) persuade someone to have sex with you, maybe using words, but also using dinner, champagne, music, lighting.

schlong (n) slang word for a penis that is long and thick.

well-hung (adj) a well-hung man has a large penis. a.k.a. well-endowed.

dutiful son (coll) a good son who does his duty, who does what is expected of him.

Note

Löwenherz is German for Lionheart. It is the name of the main gay bookshop in Vienna. It has a café attached to it, and just down the same street, Burggasse, is the Sigmund Freud Museum.

Downstairs at breakfast, Casey asked Dan what he was going to do until the meeting at four.

"I don't know. What you think we can do?"

"We? I'm too old to be seen out with you. You do what you like, young man."

Dan's heart sank. He knew that Casey was really pissed off. He didn't know what to think, let alone how to say it. "I'll walk around old city and look. What about you?"

Casey, surprised that Dan even asked, "I need to put myself into therapy. Retail therapy, of course," knowing full well that Dan would have no idea what he was talking about.

Dan spent a few hours being amazed at the size and beauty of the buildings and parks and pedestrian areas, and by the Japanese and Italian tourists, the horse-drawn carriages, the shops and cafes, and the lederhosen that people really do wear. He went into the tourist office on Albertinaplatz and got a map and some brochures. He decided to go the Sigmund Freud Museum. It was quite a way, and he couldn't afford the tram fare. He had protested when Ivana put some schnitzels and biscuits and bottles of water in his backpack, but now he was grateful. When he was almost at the Museum, it started to rain quite heavily, so he stood in the entrance of a café and waited for the rain to stop.

Out of the blue, Andreas tapped him on the shoulder and said, "We have to stop meeting like this!"

"What are you doing here?"

"Our gay bookshop is attached to this café." Andreas invited Dan in for a coffee.

"Our bookshop?"

"Yes, I have a finger in this little pie. Where's our mutual friend? Out the back?"

"No, he's at the pension, I think. We had a bit of a domestic."

"Go on."

"Well, there's only one bed in the room…"

"Say no more."

"I'm sorry to ask, but could you lend me some money? I'll give it back next week."

"It's that bad, is it?"

"I don't know. But I don't want to get stuck."

"Here you go."

"Thank you. I was just on my way to the Freud Museum."

"Are you hoping to learn something about yourself there?"

"I've been having strange dreams recently," Dan said in a dry, low voice, "full of strange men with pistols in their pockets, pointing their strange weapons at me. I thought Dr. Freud could interpret these dreams for me."

While Andreas didn't know if Dan was pulling his leg, he did think that some of the photography books in his bookshop might provide some answers.

Back in his normal voice, Dan continued. "At four we've got a meeting with some grand old man. I'm supposed to be the interpreter. I don't know why he didn't ask you."

"Aha! Mixing business with pleasure. Who's the man?"

"Some Hermann something."

"Wienerwinkel, by any chance?"

"Probably. Casey's German pronunciation isn't great."

"He knows I don't approve of Herr W, that's why. Casey is trying to get him to publish some of his fiction in German."

"Casey writes fiction?"

"Don't tell him I told you. You have to act completely surprised."

"I won't have to act. This whole weekend has been one surprise after another. We saw *Traviata* last night. I thought I was going to die, not Violetta! Then Casey tried to seduce me. Now he's not talking to me. And along the way I saw his schlong. Erect!"

"Yes, you'd need a license for it, wouldn't you?"

"At least. Ah, to be so well-hung," sighed Dan.

"I wish it were mine and he had a better one," Andreas said.

"Don't even go there. Where are you staying?"

"Hotel Mama's."

"How nice for you. Cooking, washing, and ironing included?"

"Of course."

"One must be a dutiful son," Dan said, winking.

Andreas gave Dan a warm and tender smile, and kissed him on the forehead. "You're going to make someone very happy, one day."

18 Moving House

Vocabulary

stressed out (adj) very worried, nervous, in a panic.

halls of residence (compound noun) student accommodation provided by universities.

fair game (noun) when you say that someone or something is fair game, you mean that it is OK to criticise them, attack them, seduce them.

mature (adj) people behave like adults: they show that they are emotionally developed.

Dan was stressed out because the end of the semester was approaching, and he had papers to write and tests to study for. And now he had to find new accommodation, for which he could hardly afford the time, let alone the money. He couldn't live at Ivana's, partly because of her grandmother and partly because her brother would be returning soon from two years in London. No-one in the halls of residence was able to offer him room at this time of year. When he asked Andreas, he reminded him that he hadn't repaid the little Vienna loan.

"Do you think that I should provide for you because you are an attractive young guy and I am gay? If you were my partner, my generosity would know no bounds. You are attractive, intelligent, cultured, and well-mannered. But you are also young, straight, and terribly naïve. And anyway, I'm packing up this flat soon as I'm going to be in Vienna for the whole summer. You could try Dominic. Garry has to leave soon for the UK. He's going home to teach all summer."

Dan hadn't considered that, especially after what he saw on the kitchen floor a month ago. He asked anyway, but their relationship was not easy at the moment. Garry knew that Dan's presence would drive Dominic crazy. Dan was very unhappy about the price he had to pay for being so attractive. "You could try Casey," Dominic suggested.

"Not after *Wien*. Terrible situation now. I still clean his flat, but he don't talk to me. Worst is, he don't look at me."

"Let me speak to him," Dominic offered. He rang him then and there and told Casey "…to grow up, to learn some forgiveness, and to stop treating every pretty young thing as fair game. He is more mature than you are. And anyway, admit it, you'd love to have him there."

So Dan was given keys, and he moved into Casey's spare bedroom two days later. He stood in front of the fireplace and listened as Casey explained the rules. He helped himself to the fruit from the Portuguese ceramic fruit bowl and pretended to listen to Casey's ridiculous list of rules and conditions. The main issue was that he wouldn't be paid in cash for his work.

Dan took the last cherry from the fruit bowl. Casey looked from the boy's eyes to the cherry and back again. He smiled and said, "Can I take your cherry?" just as Dan was opening his mouth.

"No, you can't," Dan replied as it disappeared. "Have a peach," he suggested as he tossed one gently across to Casey.

"Do I dare to eat a peach?" Casey said as he caught it. He looked into the boy's eyes and thought, *You have no idea, do you?*

19 Au Pairs Come in Pairs

Vocabulary

prodigal son a young man who has left his family in order to do something that the family is not happy about, and returns home feeling sorry for what he has done, and is greeted warmly.

build (n) body type. Someone's build can be petite, normal, big etc.

aura (u.n.) a special feeling or character that a person or place seems to have.

au pair (n) foreigner who lives with a family and looks after the children or cleans the house in return for meals, a room and a small payment.

discretion is the noun form of *discrete*. When you are discrete, you do not give away any personal information about other people, and you are careful about people's feelings.

straightforward (adj) uncomplicated, simple.

pocket money (compound noun) money for spending on your own personal things, typically given to teenagers.

soothe (vb) to make something less painful, to reduce stress. Can be a massage or words, for example.

compared starkly (coll) in a stark comparison one of the things looks quite bad.

Dan was invited to a special dinner at Ivana's to welcome home the prodigal son. Ivana had only ever referred to him as "my brother", and Dan was surprised to learn that his name was Ivan. Their parents had named them Ivana and Ivan. Their mother explained that they thought they would only be able to have one child, and that their father had wanted the traditional family name to continue. Dan was even more surprised at how similar the siblings looked. They had the same eyes and hair, and very similar faces. Most of all, they shared an aura. Dan felt he knew Ivan the moment they met.

Ivan spent most of the evening answering questions about London, being an au pair, and the Robinson family, while describing the photos he was passing around. Grandmother could only admire Ivan's growth spurt. "We sent them a twig and they sent us a tree," she smiled at her daughter. He had put on about 15 kgs

Dan recalled how much the Englishmen ate at that dinner party he had served at, and wondered if all English people ate so much. This would explain why Ivan had put on the weight that was quite obvious from the photos.

But Grandmother was even more interested in his luck with the opposite sex. Ivan smiled and nodded but said little. She was amused by her grandson's discretion, and didn't really believe that he had not enjoyed some sort of relationship the whole time he was in London. The lack of another person in the photos told Grandmother that he was hiding something.

Dan wanted to know how much English Ivan already knew, how much money he had saved, and how he organised the trip. The answers were straightforward – the year after finishing secondary school, he had attended a one-year full-time English course. As for money, just the bus fare from Brno to London and a bit of pocket money. Ivan added that Ivana had been saving up a bit by cleaning flats.

"Saving up for what?" Dan asked.

"The Robinsons are looking forward to her coming very much. She's moving straight into my old room, as soon as they get back from their summer house in France."

"Moving in? For how long?" Dan glared at her. It was immediately clear to everyone that she hadn't told him. They had never even discussed the "semester abroad" that language students in particular undertake.

"In August. For two years." Dan felt like he'd been kicked in the gut. He swallowed. He stared at her in disbelief. Ivana put her hand on his shoulder and apologised for not having told him sooner, but, "there never seemed to be a right moment."

Ivan put his hand on Dan's other shoulder and said that the time would go quickly. "And you can visit her. They have a great big house with a garden and a pool." They both stroked his back in gentle, soothing strokes. The images of such luxury compared starkly with the three-room flat they were currently sitting in. Mother and grandmother had two single beds in one room. Ivan and Ivana likewise. And the combined dining/living room just had a little kitchen corner.

At the end of the evening, Ivana and Ivan walked Dan to the tram stop. The news had come so out of the blue that he didn't know how he felt. Ivana squeezed his hand and said, "Come on, it's not so bad – we've got phones and email. We could even get web cameras. And anyway, Ivan's here. He will look after you." Ivan put his arm around Dan's shoulder and promised that he would.

20 Beautiful Material

Vocabulary

armpit (n) place under your arm where your arm joins your body. Most women shave their armpits. Some men too.

tickle (vb) touch someone lightly with your fingers, usually to make them laugh.

doesn't come cheap (phrase) an ironic expression meaning that something is more expensive than expected.

landlord (n) a person or organization that owns a building or an area of land. Others pay them to use it.

poke him in the ribs (verb phrase) push your finger quickly into someone's chest, usually to make them notice something or to stop them from doing or saying something.

stubble (u.n.) the short hair on a guy's face when he doesn't shave. Designer stubble is quite common in advertising.

an advance an attempt to start something with someone.

It didn't take very long for Dan to get used to living with Casey. He got used to the framed photographs by Robert Vano, Gerhard Hámor, Bruce Weber, et al. on the walls, and the DVDs and gay magazines lying around. He would even open them from time to time. He didn't mind the occasional massage when Casey would have him sit on the rug between his legs in front of the couch. Casey always seemed to have massage cream at hand and would rub it into the tops of his shoulders, his neck, and his armpits, which tickled a bit, but it was nice.

Otherwise Dan was busy studying, often in a library. He would have lunch in the university dining hall and dinner at Ivana's. After an early dinner in early summer, there was still plenty of daylight left, so he and Ivan and Ivana would go for a walk in the parks and forests or around the lake and chat away for hours. Dan found that he was really enjoying Ivan's company, which was strange because he hadn't made any good friends since he had left home and started university.

On one occasion, Dan turned up at their flat wearing a new shirt. Ivan admired it and asked Dan if he'd got lucky.

"What do you mean?" Dan asked.

"Well, Free Willy doesn't come cheap," Ivan answered, having recognised the brand at 100 paces.

"It's Casey's," Ivana said. "Dan's employer-landlord."

"He lets you wear his clothes!?"

"He might if I asked him."

"Well, it's beautiful material." And Ivan ran his open hand across Dan's chest.

"Hey, stop that," Dan said jokingly, poking him in the ribs. He was not expecting his fingers to press into a layer of spongy body fat.

"Whatever you say, chubby bubby," Dan said with a huge grin spreading across his face.

"What's not to like?" Ivan poked him back. Ivana left the children to play and went to help in the kitchen. Dan poked Ivan again, and Ivan grabbed his hand and held it. They both froze. Ivan loosened his grip a little and ran his other hand over Dan's chest again.

"Beautiful material," he whispered, looking into Dan's eyes. Dan's eyes looked back at a face that seemed to flicker between Ivana's and Ivan's. He ran his hand across Ivan's cheek, but when he felt the light stubble, his hand flicked away as if he'd got a little electric shock.

That night after dinner when they went for their walk, Dan was warmer and more loving towards Ivana than usual. At one stage, he asked Ivan to watch out for passers-by when he took her a little way into the forest. Not for the first time recently, she rejected his advances.

21 Class Reunion

Vocabulary

post-coital (adj) after sex, e.g. a post-coital cigarette.

clap (vb) at the end of a concert, for example, everyone claps, making a noise with their hands.

slap (vb) hit with your open hand, especially slap someone in the face.

class reunion (compound noun) is an event at which people who were in the same class at school get together.

cautiously (adv) in a careful way, avoiding risks.

bark (vb) talk aggressively, like a dog barking.

snack (n) something you eat between main meals.

goodies (n) something nice to eat.

When Dan got back to the flat, he was surprised to hear Casey in the middle of a wild lovemaking session. This was a first. Dan tiptoed into the kitchen, poured himself a glass of wine, and found a plate of cheese and olives that he took into the living room. He sat down and listened in the dark. He didn't try to imagine who the performers were or what they were actually doing, rather he just bathed in the sounds of passion. It was obviously coming from people far more experienced than he was, for his own lovemaking was never so intense. Nor so long. He was finishing his third glass of slowly-sipped wine when Casey emerged, following his post-coital semi-flaccid cock, and turned on the living room light. Dan stood up, smiled, and mimed clapping.

"What the fucking fuck's fuck are you doing in my shirt?" Casey shouted.

"What? This is my shirt," called the voice from the bedroom. Casey marched across the room to Dan and grabbed the glass of wine out of his hand and slapped him hard across the face. "You are unbelievable."

"Thank you," the voice replied. "You are good, too." Casey was waiting for some response from Dan. Dan was already in shock, but when he looked across at the figure emerging from the bedroom, he simply said, "Good evening, Mr Tošenovsky," in Czech.

Marek looked up. "Dan, what are you doing here?"

"I live here."

"You two know each other?" Casey was quite surprised.

"Yes, he was my PE teacher at school."

"PE teacher?" Casey looked at Marek. "I hope you took his course in foreskin management!" How disgusting, thought Dan.

"But I have my own fitness centre now," Marek told Dan. "Do you two live together?"

"Yes," said Dan.

"No," said Casey. "He's just staying in the spare room for a while. A very short while. He's moving out very soon."

"After my exams, I will go back to my parents' place for the summer."

"And how are you liking university?"

"It's great, I guess. How is your business?"

"Excuse me," Casey interrupted. "Do we have to have this fucking class reunion now?"

"I don't suppose you'd be interested in a little three-way action, by any chance?" Marek asked, direct, yet cautious.

"I'm not gay," said Dan.

"He didn't ask you if you were gay. Fucking heterosexual pigeon-holing. He was just wondering if you'd like a bit of action," barked Casey.

Dan explained to Marek that he had met Casey through his girlfriend who was cleaning here. "And now I'm the cleaner and secretary and everything."

"Enough of this bullshit, for fuck's sake! He hasn't done a thing since he moved in. Look at all these CD covers all over the room! And he's just drunk a bottle of wine and eaten the snack I'd prepared for us. And now he's even wearing my clothes. Little shit."

Dan hated being in such a situation, especially in front of a former teacher who had thought the sun shone out of him. "Well at least I'm wearing clothes."

"Are you telling us to get dressed? Whose flat is this, you little prick? And anyway, you are wearing my clothes! Now give me my shirt back." Dan went into striptease mode, and Casey's cock started to grow. Dan threw the shirt across the room and it caught on Casey's erection.

"Bravo!" shouted Marek. Even though he didn't like the way Casey treated Dan, he was enjoying the little show. He had had enough of

Casey's talent for the evening, but he could never have enough of Dan. He has been wanking over him for years.

"Now, go and open another bottle of wine and get some more goodies." Dan had no choice but to follow orders. His world was turning upside down. He was already in the kitchen when Casey called from the living room, "And take your jeans off!" Dan was crying on the inside and shaking on the outside.

22 Anyone for Tennis?

Vocabulary

shift (n) period within a 24 hr day when it is planned you will work. Many factories have three 8 hr shifts a day.

pent-up energy (coll) when something is pent-up it is held inside and not expressed, typically energy and emotions.

aggression (uncount n.) spoken or physical behaviour which seems threatening or involves harm to someone or something.

talent scout (compound noun) person looking for suitably talented people, actors and models in particular.

slim pickings (compound noun) when you have little choice.

defend (vb) protect someone or something against attack or criticism.

outburst (n) sudden forceful expression of emotion, especially anger, usually unexpected.

wick (n) part of a candle that is lit with a match. When an explosive, such as dynamite, has a short wick, it explodes quickly. When we say that a person has a short wick, we mean that they get angry very suddenly because of something that is not very important.

shower someone or something with ... give a lot of something in a generous way. Also: shower attention on something.

compensate (vb) for something by providing something good or useful after someone has failed or something been damaged or lost.

Notes

Don't go there in this context means, don't think about it, stop talking about it, do not continue with this thought.

Slowly slowly catchee monkey is a phrase that means, if you are patient and take the right steps, you will get what you want.

a heart of gold (fixed phrase) a way of saying that someone is very kind and generous.

au contraire a French expression meaning, *on the contrary*: used in English by people who enjoy language. *Mein Leibling*: the German phrase for *my dear.*

párek is the Czech word for *frankfurter* as used in hot dogs. It rhymes closely with Marek, the Czech equivalent of Mark.

The next time Casey got home from squash at Marek's gym, he told Dan that Marek had some part-time work for him. "Don't worry, it's a straight-friendly gym." Despite being busy with his seminar papers and end of semester exams, Dan decided he could squeeze in several shifts a week. At the end of his third shift, Marek invited him to a round of squash. Dan had never played before, but he accepted. He was certainly aware that he was not getting enough physical activity these days. They played long and hard. Dan seemed to be releasing a lot of pent-up energy and the aggression surprised Marek.

The only other people playing at that hour were Dominic and Garry. When Dominic and Casey had been a couple, they had played there regularly. Dominic finds saunas a great place to talent scout for his films – even slim pickings can bear fruit. On the other hand, Garry's only involvement in sport to date was his passion for football and cricket on the telly. He had certainly never played squash.

After their hard-fought duels on the courts, the four players headed for the sauna and Jacuzzi. Out of the blue, Andreas turned up following the ball he was hitting on the floor with his racket. "It seems I've missed all the action," he moaned.

"*Au contraire, mein Liebling!*" Dominic whispered.

The five men all stripped and climbed into the Jacuzzi. As Dominic was admiring the facilities, he remembered thinking what an ideal film location it would be. Now that he knew the manager, he decided to ask him if there would be any chance of making a film there.

"It'd be a great honour," Marek answered. "I don't suppose you could create a little part for me, do you?"

"Oh, I'm sure we could squeeze you in," Dominic replied.

"... to some tight little student arse," added Andreas as he turned and looked at Dan.

"Don't even go there," Garry warned.

"Slowly slowly catchee monkey," Dominic said through a strange smile.

Dan and Marek started chatting in Czech about their hometown, its local celebrities, and the school where they had been student and teacher. As the conversation inevitably turned to Casey, Marek expressed his surprise that Dan could live with him. When the others heard the name Casey, they entered the conversation and it continued in English. "After all, he is so aggressive towards you," said Marek.

To everyone's surprise, Dan defended Casey, saying that he had a heart of gold and wouldn't hurt a fly. "He just has some outbursts from time to time, but apart from that..."

"He has a short wick," Garry threw in. They all laughed. When they got to the showers, Dan couldn't help noticing that his was the shortest wick of all, despite all the love and attention he had showered upon it over the years. He even wondered if being well-hung made someone gay. *Perhaps it's Darwinian*, he thought. God's way of compensating them for all the difficulties they meet, living in a narrow-minded society.

There were six shower heads and two soap dispensers. The room was filling up with steam but not so much that they couldn't all study in great detail and respectful silence the beauty of Dan's face, his chest with its newly discovered sensitive nipples, the perfectly flat and hairless torso, the Adonis Cut leading the eye towards his lovely little penis and balls resting in that beautiful black pubic nest, the elegant calves, muscular shins, and his blessed delicate feet. Dominic recalled a line from the Ted Hughes poem, "A March Calf": "half of him legs". Andreas was reminded of a Greek statue. Garry remembered his own body fifteen years earlier. Marek remembered the even younger Dan he had closely watched as he developed during his high school years. Ah! What memories.

As admirable (or offensive, according to Casey) as young beauty is, Andreas is a man's man. And in present company, that meant Dominic under the shower opposite. As Dominic's cock started to respond to Andreas's attention, Marek became interested, too. Standing on Dominic's left, Marek started to make eye contact with the growing schlong. The only thing Dominic could do now was to turn to his lover on his right and start washing his back. Marek thoughtfully offered Dan a good back wash. When Dan declined, Andreas accepted. When Garry said, "your turn," Dominic turned around and Dan saw him fully erect. He then noticed Marek's and Andreas's, too. When Dan felt his own cock starting to grow, he made a discreet exit.

"Well, if it weren't for the short wick, he'd be perfect," Garry fired the first shot.

"I thought you said he had a bit to play with down there," Dominic reminded Garry without a hint of a smile.

"No, it's not much of a schlong, is it?" said Andreas.

"More of a shlort, really," replied Dominic.

"Aber das ist nicht so schlimm," said Andreas adding yet another layer of word play.

"Well gentlemen, I'm sure I could learn to live with it," Marek said, as he turned around and let Andreas start washing his back.

"Quality, gentlemen, not quantity," said Dominic.

"But you wouldn't cast him in a film, would you?" asked Marek.

"Not the kind of films he makes," Garry answered for him.

"I suppose we could make a teacher-student film," Dominic said, thinking aloud. "Now, who could play the teacher, I wonder?"

Marek smiled at Dominic. "Do you really think that size matters that much?" he asked. As a PE teacher, Marek had seen a lot of growing boys.

"You can do more with more," Andreas said.

"It's better box office," Garry said. "Have you seen that film with Casey?"

"And how do you think Dan feels," Marek continued, "surrounded by your handsome English and Austrian schlongs?"

"Don't forget your own *parek*, Marek." Andreas rhymed as he squeezed it.

"It's not a contest of international dimensions," Garry threw in with a smile.

"Let's face it, we're all size queens!" laughed Andreas.

"Oh yes it is," said Dominic returning to Garry's comment. "It's the European Schlong Contest."

"That is so bad!" shrieked Andreas.

"Wicked, wicked, wicked!' said Garry breathily, shaking his head at this stroke of genius.

23 Exit, Pursued by a Bear with a Sore Head

Vocabulary

obsessive need (coll) so interested in or worried about something that you behave differently from your normal ways.

lock up (phrasal vb) lock all the doors when you close a shop, for example.

favour kind thing that you do for someone

shoot his load (verb phrase) when semen leaves your penis. a.k.a. ejaculate, cum, blow.

tongue-in-cheek (adj) something said "tongue-in-cheek" is not meant seriously. Just kidding.

rim (u.n.) the edge of something especially round, e.g. the rim of a glass, the Pacific Rim.

familiar ring (coll) something that you have heard before does not sound new or strange. It has a familiar ring.

A couple of weeks later and the semester over, Dan was getting ready to go back to his parents' for the summer. The plan was for Ivana to spend a week there with him in their family cottage in the woods by a large lake, the place of his happiest childhood memories. She had been there once before. The following week, she would go to London.

Dan's last shift at the fitness centre was quiet. Ivan turned up out of the blue for a game of squash with him after closing. Dan wondered if he had come to shed a few of those extra kilos. Ivan had an OJ at the bar and waited till the last customers left. He had played a bit of tennis in London with the Robinsons and was no stranger to squash either. He roundly defeated Dan time and again. Dan had not suspected that Ivan would have such an obsessive need to win, and it was starting to get on his nerves. It showed a lack of support for an unmatched rival. "Come on, it's just a game," he said. This made Ivan more aggressive and he played even harder as he repeated Dan's words in a girly, sing-song way. The change in his personality was not unlike road rage.

Dan had had enough and announced he was hitting the showers. "No, you're not."

"I'm not?" Dan glared at him and waited for an explanation. And just as suddenly, Ivan snapped back to his charming self.

"It's late, time to lock up. Let's go for a beer."

"But I stink," Dan said. "I've been working all day and now this game." As they changed into their jeans and T-shirts, Ivan started to complain about the pains in his shoulder. "Serves you right."

"Thanks for the sympathy."

"You get what you deserve." Casey's flat was just around the corner, and Dan wanted to show it off. They could hang out there for a while and have a beer or two. Ivan had never seen such an impressive flat in Brno.

"Now can I have a shower, Master?" Dan got undressed, folded his clothes, wrapped a towel around himself and headed for the bathroom.

In a rather nervous voice, Ivan said, "You couldn't give this shoulder a massage, could you? It's killing me." He took his T-shirt off and lay down on Dan's bed.

"No. Do some stretching exercises while I have a shower. And don't lie on my bed in your day clothes." As quick as a flash, Ivan was totally naked. "Please, I'd love a massage."

"Please? Did you say please? You little shit." Suddenly Dan saw an opportunity to take revenge for the squash match. Ivan was lying face down on the bed so Dan didn't mind sitting on his butt and really pounding his shoulders. The smell of Ivan almost made him feel drunk. There was a hint of Ivana, the sweet smell of sweat, and a little something that he couldn't quite place.

Ivan was not expecting such a forceful and delightful beating. It was wonderful. "Further down," he urged. Dan squeezed some oil onto his back. "You're a very good masseur. Keep going." Dan ended up massaging his buttocks, which separated enough in the process to bring a look of wonder to Dan's eyes. Ivan's breathing told him what to do next. He squeezed a little oil on it and gently massaged it. Ivan raised his slightly chubby buttocks and Dan wondered if he was meant to go further.

"I'm going to have a shower," he said, hoping to avoid a "situation".

"No, let me return the favour," Ivan said quickly. He turned over and pulled himself out from between Dan's legs. Dan couldn't help noticing Ivan's erection and how similar its dimensions were to his own. According to Dan's recent theory, this meant that Ivan couldn't be gay, either. Ivan playfully pushed Dan down on the bed and twisted his legs so that he was lying face down. He rested his weight on his wrists in front of Dan's shoulders. He started to breathe warm air onto Dan's back, and then he started drawing large figures of eight with his tongue. As he moved further and further down, he put his hands beside Dan's waist. He licked into the dimples of Dan's cheeks and then between them until his tongue met Dan's hole.

"Stop it!" Dan cried. "I like it!" Then less dramatically, he said, "I love it." Ivan froze. And as the weight of waiting lifted, he added word by word, "I love you," and shot his load into the sheets. Ivan flicked Dan's whole body over. Their faces were only centimetres apart.

"You're just talking out of your arse," Ivan whispered through a sweet tongue-in-cheek smile.

"There was something the moment I saw you," Dan said with tears in his eyes. "But I didn't realise what it was. Kiss me." Ivan leaned down and ran his tongue around the rim of Dan's lips. Dan lay completely passive. "You want take my cherry?" Dan said, speaking English suddenly.

"There's nothing I'd like more," Ivan whispered back. "And if that's the only English you know, I'll love you even more."

"I thought that's what he meant," Dan said, returning to Czech.

"Casey?"

"Who else?" Dan continued, "You're very welcome to my cherry. But not here, not in his flat. I'm going home to my parents' tomorrow. Can you come the day after? We'll have our cottage in the woods all to ourselves. You can teach me all day and all night. It'll be beautiful."

Ivan was reluctant to give up the opportunity that lay in his hands here and now. But on the other hand, he was totally seduced by the romanticism of the boy virgin declaring his love. He obviously had no choice but to agree, even though he half-feared Dan was just saying this as a way of getting out of it altogether. Ivan agreed by kissing Dan, stroking his hair, and rubbing their two sticks together. My, what sparks!

And then a third much older voice shouted, "What the fucking fuck's fuck is going on here? Who the fuck are you? And what the fuck do you think you are doing in my flat, you fucking lout!" Dan felt this had a familiar ring to it. He looked up at Casey with a silly smile. "And who might you be, young man?"

"I'm sorry," Ivan said, his whole body shaking. Casey looked back at Dan and waited for an explanation.

"I'm sorry, Casey. He's my boyfriend and he speaks English. He's Ivana's brother."

"Ivana with a prick, if you ask me, you little prick! You have no right to bring anyone into this flat. Get the fuck out of here. And don't come back." As Dan was about to close the door, he asked Casey if they could still be friends. Casey shot back, "I've got enough friends, thank you. Now piss off!" and slammed the door.

24 On the Home Straight

Vocabulary

crackling a lot of short, dry, sharp sounds, like fireworks.

bonhomie (u.n.) friendly and happy atmosphere. A French word we use in English.

it never crossed my mind (verb phrase) didn't think of something because there was no reason to.

take something for granted believe something to be the truth without even thinking about it. He took it for granted that ...

as an afterthought (fixed phrase) an idea, thought or plan which was not originally intended but comes at a later time.

The following day, Dan packed up and went home to his parents. His father met him at the station and they went straight out to the cottage for a long afternoon of eating and drinking and chatting, and a bit of gardening and tennis. *The Marriage of Figaro* was crackling out of the old gramophone. It was a lovely afternoon of family bonhomie.

Dan waited for the inevitable questions about Ivana and her family.

"She is still coming in two weeks, as planned. But then she's going to England for two years to work as an *au pair*. Her brother has just come back and she's taking over at the same family."

"Oh dear, that'll leave a gap."

"I know, but it seems I've found someone to fill it."

"That was quick, dear."

"Well, I met her brother a few weeks ago. And I think I'm in love. I can't believe it really. I know some gay people but it never crossed my mind that I could be one."

"Falling in love with a friend doesn't make you gay, son."

"I've only known him for a couple of weeks, Dad. He's not my friend. That's what I realise now – Ivana's been my best friend."

"That should've been a warning to you, don't you think, dear?"

"I didn't think so. But there were times when I really knew that it wasn't quite right. There was something missing."

"Well, of course there was, dear." Dan's mother smiled at her husband.

"It's just that it's come so out of the blue."

"Really, dear?" said his mother, sounding surprised. "You could have asked us."

"You can't have known before me. That's impossible." He looked from father to mother and back again. "Seems not!" He sighed. "I really thought I was in love with Ivana but my feelings for her are nothing compared to what I feel for him."

"I hope you've told him," his father said seriously.

"Look, this all happened only a few days ago. But he knows."

"Never take that for granted, son. It's the biggest mistake you can make."

Dan squeezed his father's hand and thanked him.

"So what's his name?"

"Ivan."

"Family name, then, is it? Lucky we didn't call your sister Daniela!"

"And when do we get to meet the lucky young man?" his mother asked in time-honoured fashion.

"Tomorrow. I hope you don't mind."

"Well, we would have liked to spend some time with just you," she said.

"We don't see much of you any more," said his father. "But if this young man is so important to you, what can we say? We look forward to meeting him." As an afterthought, his father threw in, "And I hear you can get married, these days."

"Calm down, you two. We've only ever kissed."

25 An Apple a Day

Vocabulary

rough and tumble (fixed phrase) like children when they run around, falling, pushing and pulling each other.

spoil (vb) treat someone very or too well, especially by being extremely generous.

hit the sack (idiom) go to bed.

a **nip in the air** (idiom) the weather is a little cold and it is time to put another piece of clothing.

hand-me-downs (n) usually a piece of clothing which someone has given to a younger relative or friend often because it is too small, i.e. they have grown out of it.

grope (vb) using your hands to find something you can't see or to find you way, usually when in the dark.

spread-eagled (adv) lying with arms and legs stretched out, usually on a bed. Try it!

stand akimbo (adv) arms are bent at the elbows and the hands are on the hips. Try it!

drift off (phrasal vb) fall asleep slowly.

dangle (vb) hang loosely.

The following afternoon, Dan and his father picked Ivan up from the station. While Ivan was throwing his backpack in the boot, Father whispered through a smile, "Ivana with stubble and a prick!"

"I've heard that before. He's beautiful, isn't he?"

"He could lose a bit of weight."

"What's not to like? He's gorgeous."

They drove out to the cottage and had a wonderful afternoon. They got on like a house on fire. Then the parents went back to town, as they had to get up early for work the next morning.

"Be good!" were his mother's standard parting words.

"I'll be excellent. Don't you worry about that!"

The boys drank on. They chased each other round the garden, rough and tumble on the freshly cut grass. When Ivan stretched up to pick an apple, Dan pulled his shorts down. Ivan stepped out of them completely and said to him, "I think we are going to be very happy." He passed the apple to Dan as if it were a religious object. Dan held it between his teeth and leaned forward and they bit into it at the same time. They wrapped their arms around each other and took a bite, then let the apple fall to the ground. "An apple a day keeps me happy and gay," Ivan said in English. He bent down as if to pick up the apple, but slid Dan's shorts off instead, then poked his tongue into his navel.

"Hey, stop that."

"Yeah, yeah, 'Stop it! I like it!' I know."

"No, it really tickles."

"Poor baby!" Dan ran off and half hid behind the walnut tree. Ivan chased him and they danced around the great trunk. Dan climbed up onto one of the branches as he had done all his life. Ivan followed him up and Dan jumped down into the soft grass. Ivan kept chasing him until Dan eventually ran up onto the cottage terrace. "I give up!"

he cried, and poured himself another glass of wine. Ivan picked a couple of strawberries, washed them and dropped one into Dan's wine and another into his mouth. "Cheers, chubby chaser."

"You're spoiling me."

"This is just the beginning." Ivan sat on the old wooden chair, still warm from the day's sun, and Dan threw his feet into Ivan's lap. Ivan took Dan's big toe between his thumb and index finger and started, "This little piggy went to market." When he got to "all the way home", his ten fingers danced up Dan's legs as far as they could. Dan leaned forward and caught the fingers between his own. Their foreheads rested together and they rubbed noses like good Eskimos.

"Let's hit the sack," Ivan said in English.

"The what?"

"Let's go to bed," Ivan explained.

"No, it's too early. I'm not tired at all. Are you?" Dan said, returning to Czech.

"Well, I wasn't actually thinking of sleeping."

"Have another drink, you sex maniac." Dan refilled their glasses. They chatted for a while about their summer plans, Ivana, their parents, and their studies. Then Dan wanted to know about being gay in England and what things were like in London. About picking people up or whatever. Ivan was far from inexperienced and was able to answer all of Dan's questions and more. Dan almost wished he were going to the Robinsons instead of Ivana.

The sun was now in the land of Nod and the almost-full moon was floating in a sea of stars. There was a bit of a nip in the air and Dan announced he was going upstairs to put his pyjamas on. "Pyjamas!?" Ivan scoffed. A minute later, the toilet flushed and then there was silence.

Ivan sat on the terrace, lightly stroking his skin, which the cool night air had turned to goose bumps. He had never welcomed his sister's hand-me-downs until now – and for Dan, he silently thanked her.

Eventually he groped his way upstairs to find what he was half-expecting. The sun was not alone in the land of Nod. Dan was spread-eagle on a big old mattress on the floor, illuminated only by the moon, and snoring lightly. Ivan stood over him, arms akimbo. He whispered, "You bastard!" and smiled. He lay down beside Dan and rested his head on his abdomen. He kissed his navel and threw one leg over one of Dan's. His fingers slowly combed Dan's little black bush, till he, too, fell asleep.

Many hours later, as Dan slowly woke up, he groped around and found himself alone. He stood up and looked out the window. Ivan was shaking the last droplets of a piss against the apple tree. Dan watched him stretch his full torso as he picked some apples and then some cherries. He admired his butt as he bent over to pick some to-matoes, and smiled at the sight of Ivan's dangling cock as he crouched down to pick strawberries. This moving kaleidoscope of Ivan's body parts was motivating some of his own body parts to look forward to showing off. Dan lay back down on the bed and pressed himself into the mattress. He was still feeling a bit funny from all the wine, and now the mid-morning sun was beating down on him. He drifted back into a half-sleep.

He didn't hear Ivan's footsteps or feel the silky-skinned cherry Ivan rested on his crack. But he did hear the camera click as Ivan created the cover picture for this book. *Quite a cute arse, haven't I?* he thought to himself and wondered why the author had spent more ink on his little cock than on his silky peach-fuzz arse. He reached around to feel what he could feel, but his hand brushed against Ivan's *párek*. Ivan wrapped his boyfriend's fingers around it. Dan moved his other hand towards his arse but Ivan caught his wrist. With his teeth, Ivan then lifted the cherry from between Dan's buttocks. As Dan tried to look around, Ivan dangled the offending fruit in front of him.

"You're taking my cherry, aren't you?" Dan asks.

"Every good boy deserves fruit," Ivan smiled.

After a summer of a thousand first loves, the boys moved back to the city to continue their studies. Instead of looking any further for accommodation, it was agreed that Dan could fill Ivana's empty bed, sharing a room with Ivan. There was much to look forward to.

Afterword

If you are a learner of English, and you have not yet been to the e-learning course associated with this story, it's not too late. You can practice the vocabulary, discuss ideas and references in the book, and meet other people who are also gay learners of English.

Send an email to gymnopinfo@gmail.com with the User Name you'd like to use, your first and last names and your email address.

Hope to see you soon.

Calvin Corvidian

www.ingramcontent.com/pod-product-compliance
Lightning Source LLC
Chambersburg PA
CBHW020312290526
45784CB00003B/1485